100

THINGS TO DO IN
INDIANAPOLIS
BEFORE YOU
DIE

Photo Courtesy of Mike Wiltrout, Indiana Landmarks

2ⁿᵈ Edition

100

THINGS TO DO IN
INDIANAPOLIS
BEFORE YOU
DIE

ASHLEY PETRY

REEDY PRESS

Library of Congress Control Number: 2018936119

ISBN: 9781681061481

Design by Jill Halpin

Printed in the United States of America
18 19 20 21 22 5 4 3 2 1

Please note that websites, phone numbers, addresses, and company names are
subject to change or cancellation. We did our best to relay the most accurate
information available, but due to circumstances beyond our control, please do not
hold us liable for misinformation. When exploring new destinations, please do your
homework before you go.

CONTENTS

● ●

Music and Entertainment

• •

Sports and Recreation

Culture and History

• •

Shopping and Fashion

PREFACE

It's been three years since the first edition of *100 Things to Do in Indianapolis Before You Die* hit the shelves, and writing this second edition has made me realize how much has changed. Many beloved restaurants have closed, only to be replaced by a fascinating array of new options. We've lost some storied retail shops, but it's hard to keep track of all the new breweries, distilleries, and coffeehouses. Our theater companies have invested heavily in refurbishing old spaces and building new venues, even as the indie arts scene has shifted to more affordable neighborhoods. Several popular events have been discontinued, but we've barely noticed—our calendars are packed with the new ones.

In the end, nearly seventy of the first edition's hundred entries had to be updated, rewritten, or simply replaced. This is a whole new book—a fitting tribute to our ever-changing city. A few years ago, Lonely Planet dubbed Indianapolis "America's most surprising city," and it keeps on surprising even those of us who live here.

This book, like the last one, is a love letter to my lifelong home. For visitors, it showcases the city's top sights—and gives you reasons to keep coming back. And residents will find gems here too, from a peaceful evensong service to a clamorous percussion museum, from a tucked-away stargazing experience to a workshop on surviving in the wild.

To the people and places mentioned in this book: For nearly fifteen years, it has been my privilege as a travel writer to hear your stories, to unintentionally memorize your addresses, and to spread the word about everything you've done to shape this wonderful city. Thank you, thank you, thank you.

Ashley Petry

ACKNOWLEDGMENTS

First, overwhelming gratitude to the team at Reedy Press: You put your authors first even when the warehouse was burning to the ground. Working with you has been both a genuine pleasure and a life-changing opportunity. Thank you.

Thanks also to the tourism experts, communications professionals, business owners, and others who helped me pull together the material for this book—with a special shout-out, as always, to Morgan Snyder and the incredible team at Visit Indy.

Endless thanks to the family members and friends who gamely joined me on research missions: Mom, Sarah, Aaron, Nathan, Meagan, Brooke, and of course Will and Cara, the two great lights of my life.

And most of all to Henry, who kept me organized, and Michael, who kept me fed. If everyone gets one miracle, your love and support are mine.

FOOD
AND DRINK

FIND THE SWEET SPOT
AT THE CAKE BAKE SHOP

Tucked away in a Broad Ripple cottage, this bakery is a fairyland of flowers, mirrors, twinkling lights, and over-the-top seasonal decor. But the beautiful setting never overshadows the cakes, which tempt from beneath domes of glass. The three-layer Gwendolyn's Famous Earl's Court Chocolate Cake (named for owner Gwendolyn Rogers) has appeared on Food Network's *Guilty Pleasures*, and the mint-chocolate-chip cake was recently featured in *O, the Oprah Magazine*.

Stop by for a cappuccino and a slice of cake, or check out the Cake Bake Shop's daily lunch and dinner menu, with French-inspired menu items such as quiche and croque monsieur. Afternoon tea (reservations required) features a tiered tray of finger sandwiches, pastries, fresh-baked scones sprinkled with glitter, and a selection of English teas—a perfect outing for the little princess in your life.

6515 Carrollton Ave., 317-257-2253
www.thecakebakeshop.com

TREK
THE MARTHA HOOVER TRAIL

Full disclosure: The Martha Hoover Trail isn't a real thing. I made it up. But Hoover, one of the city's most successful restaurateurs, is the brains behind a profusion of wonderful restaurants. So to taste the best of Indy, simply follow in her footsteps.

The trail starts at Café Patachou, which serves fluffy omelets and decadent broken-yolk sandwiches. (Don't miss the cinnamon toast.) Chronologically, the next stop is Petite Chou, a French-style bistro and champagne bar known for its crepes and duck-fat *pomme frites*. Next is Napolese, serving thin-crust Neapolitan pizzas with gourmet toppings. My favorite (although it's a very close call) is Public Greens, a farm-to-fork cafeteria serving healthy soups, salads, veggies, and more. (Try the quinoa chili.) The newest additions to the roster are Crispy Bird, a fancy fried-chicken joint, and Bar One Fourteen, a tiny bar with elevated cocktails. Visit all six and you win . . . nothing. It's a fake trail. But the food is its own reward.

www.patachouinc.com

FIND
YOUR FAVORITE FINE DINING

Not so long ago, fine dining in Indianapolis meant chain steak houses and . . . other chain steak houses. Not anymore. The city's restaurant renaissance has made it easy to choose a unique dining experience for special occasions.

Indy has far too many fantastic restaurants to list, so here are my personal favorites. For hip, modern menus and clever cocktails, try Black Market or Bluebeard (named after a novel by Indy native Kurt Vonnegut). For romantic ambiance, your best bets are Meridian, Mama Carolla's Old Italian Restaurant, Ocean Prime, and Tinker Street. Late Harvest Kitchen and Oakley's Bistro are chef-driven restaurants with inventive, ever-changing seasonal menus.

Other favorites include St. Elmo Steak House, the Loft at Traders Point Creamery, and the Cunningham family of restaurants (especially Livery and Vida). For other ideas, try browsing *Indianapolis Monthly* magazine's annual list of the city's best restaurants.

TOP OPTIONS FOR FINE DINING

Black Market
922 Massachusetts Ave.
317-822-6757
www.blackmarketindy.net

*Don't miss: roasted marrow bones,
daily pickles, salted-chocolate brickle*

Bluebeard
653 Virginia Ave.
317-686-1580
www.bluebeardindy.com

*Don't miss: charcuterie platters,
craft cocktails, brussels sprouts
agrodolce*

Late Harvest Kitchen
8605 River Crossing
317-663-8063
www.lateharvestkitchen.com

*Don't miss: seafood, rabbit,
potatoes Minneapolis*

Mama Carolla's Old Italian Restaurant
1031 E. Fifty-Fourth St.
317-259-9412
www.mamacarollas.com

Don't miss: lasagna, veal, tiramisu

Meridian
5694 N. Meridian St.
317-466-1111
www.meridianonmeridian.com

*Don't miss: smoked corn puree,
wild boar bolognese, duck confit*

Oakley's Bistro
1464 W. Eighty-Sixth St.
317-824-1231
www.oakleysbistro.com

*Don't miss: shrimp corndogs,
goat-cheese macaroni, seasonal salads*

Ocean Prime
8555 N. River Rd.
317-569-0975
www.oceanprimeindy.com

*Don't miss: lobster bisque,
filet mignon, the Berries and
Bubbles cocktail*

Tinker Street
402 E. Sixteenth St.
317-925-5000
www.tinkerstreetindy.com

*Don't miss: pork belly, seafood, s'more
pot de creme*

TRACK DOWN
INDY'S BEST FOOD TRUCKS

A few years into the food truck craze, some of Indy's original favorites, such as Duos and Spice Box, have graduated to brick-and-mortar locations. But you'll still find plenty of trucks—more than a hundred at last count—serving traditional street foods with a gourmet flair. Here are a few to track down:

- Caveman Truck: "Bacon > gluten" is the slogan for this truck focused on the paleo diet and "primal" cuisine.
- Chef Dan's Southern Comfort: Order up some Southern favorites, including red beans and rice, fried chicken, po'boys, and banana pudding.
- Nicey Treat: This warm-weather favorite serves all-natural popsicles in flavors such as strawberry-mint, avocado, and mango-ginger.
- Soul Sista on the Move: For food just like Grandma used to make, check out the chicken wings, pork chops, greens, sweet potatoes, and mac and cheese.

Caveman Truck, www.cavemantruck.com
Chef Dan's Southern Comfort, www.chefdansindy.com
Nicey Treat, www.niceytreat.com
Soul Sista on the Move, www.facebook.com/SoulSistaOnTheMove

REAP
THE CUNNINGHAM REWARDS

Many of Indy's most innovative restaurants have one thing in common: they're operated by the locally owned Cunningham Restaurant Group, which has fueled the city's culinary renaissance. So it makes sense to sign up for the Cunningham VIP card: you'll earn a point for every dollar you spend, and a thousand points gets you a one hundred dollar gift card.

To earn points or spend your rewards, head to the epicenter of Cunningham's creativity: Mass Ave's Bru Burger Bar has fabulous burgers. Union 50 has a seasonal menu and live music, while Mesh offers fine dining in a more intimate setting. Vida, known for its eye-catching hydroponic wall of greens, is easily a contender for the city's best restaurant. But my personal favorite is Livery, which serves Latin-inspired dishes; think empanadas, yuca fries, pork belly tacos, and churros. Other Cunningham restaurants include Stone Creek Dining Company, Boulder Creek Dining Company, Charbonos, and two eateries at the north-side Ironworks Hotel.

www.crgdining.com

TRY INDIANA'S SIGNATURE DESSERT:
SUGAR CREAM PIE

Indiana's official state pie is a simple yet delicious blend of butter, sugar, vanilla, and cream, which creates a custard-like filling. Invented by Quaker settlers in the early 1800s, the dessert was later embraced by the state's large Amish community.

My sister, Sarah, swears by the sugar cream pie at Locally Grown Gardens, and she's in good company: it's also the top-rated option on Yelp. The year-round farm market, located in SoBro, sells pies whole or by the slice.

My favorite spot for a slice of sugar cream pie is Gray Brothers Cafeteria in Mooresville. The restaurant has been in business since 1944 and serves home-style dishes, such as fried chicken and meatloaf. It gets the sugar cream pie exactly right: not too sweet, with just a hint of jiggle in the filling.

Another top pick is Lisa's Pie Shop, located north of Indianapolis in tiny Atlanta. The award-winning bakery (cash or check only) is recognized as one of the best in the nation.

Locally Grown Gardens, 1050 E. Fifty-Fourth St., 317-255-8555
www.locallygrowngardens.com

Gray Brothers Cafeteria, 555 S. Indiana St., Mooresville, 317-831-7234
www.graybroscafe.com

Lisa's Pie Shop, 5995 Hwy 31, Atlanta, 317-758-6944, www.lisaspies.com

FEEL THE BURN:
SHRIMP COCKTAIL AT ST. ELMO STEAK HOUSE

If you eat at just one restaurant in Indianapolis, it should probably be St. Elmo Steak House. In business for more than a century, the renowned Illinois Street eatery is still the best place to spot celebrities, such as racecar drivers and Indianapolis Colts players. But the real draw is the legendary shrimp cocktail, which contains so much horseradish that it can literally take your breath away. You're not a real Hoosier until your eyes water.

127 S. Illinois St., 317-635-0636
www.stelmos.com

TIP

For a more casual St. Elmo experience, check out its sister restaurant, Harry and Izzy's. You'll find locations downtown (153 S. Illinois St.), on the north side (4050 E. Eighty-Second St.), and at the Indianapolis International Airport.

PICK YOUR FAVORITE
PORK TENDERLOIN

Indiana's signature dish is the breaded pork tenderloin sandwich, featuring a pork patty pounded out so thinly that it covers the entire plate. It was invented at Nick's Kitchen in Huntington, Indiana, as an alternative to the owner's beloved German schnitzel. But if you can't make the road trip, Indy offers scads of alternatives. The only challenge is choosing your favorite. Indy's old-school hangouts, such as Indy's Historic Steer-In Restaurant and Mug n Bun, are at the top of the list. Others swear by the tenderloins at the Aristocrat Pub and Restaurant or Upland Brewing Co.'s Carmel Tap House, which also offers a vegetarian seitan version. And don't overlook the tenderloin at Nickel Plate Bar and Grill in Fishers. (My apologies to the dozens of solid options I had to leave out.)

Aristocrat Pub and Restaurant, 5212 N. College Ave., 317-283-7388
www.aristocratpub.com

Carmel Tap House, 820 E. 116th St., 317-564-3400
www.uplandbeer.com

Nickel Plate Bar and Grill, 8654 E. 116th St., 317-841-2888
www.nickelplatebarandgrill.com

EXPLORE
THE INDIANAPOLIS CITY MARKET

When the City Market opened in 1886, the sprawling complex housed vendors selling meat, cheese, produce, and other farm-fresh goods. Today, the revitalized market is known for its food kiosks, making it the perfect place to grab a quick lunch downtown, especially on weekdays when it is at its busiest and all the kiosks are open. Get a soft-baked pretzel from Pat's Philly Pretzels, a fruit tart or French macaron from Circle City Sweets, a kefir soda from Fermenti Artisan, a healthy Balance Bowl from Duos, fresh tamales from the Tamale Place, or a vegetarian seitan sandwich from Three Carrots. Circle City Soups is another popular pick, especially if its famous sweet-corn chowder is on the menu. Then, head upstairs to the Tomlinson Tap Room, where you can wash down your lunch with a selection of local microbrews.

222 E. Market St., 317-634-9266
www.indycm.com

TIP

Indiana Landmarks offers tours of the City Market catacombs, a series of dimly lit brick archways beneath the market's outdoor plaza. They're all that's left of Tomlinson Hall, an auditorium that burned to the ground in 1958.

www.indianalandmarks.org/tours

MEET YOUR FAVORITE MEAD
AT NEW DAY CRAFT

Spend just five minutes at New Day Craft's sleek tasting room in Fountain Square, and you'll understand why mead isn't just for medieval banquets anymore. Spring for a tasting flight of the light, crisp honey-based wines, such as Washington's Folly, a mead with hints of cherry and vanilla. My favorites are the seasonal varieties: autumn's Paulding Light, with a tangy cranberry flavor, and winter's Breakfast Magpie, with zings of blackberry and espresso.

Don't miss New Day's selection of hard ciders, which are just as popular as its meads. Start with the dry Gold Rush, and then try the South Cider (sweetened with honey) and the Johnny Chapman (sweetened with Indiana sorghum). Pick a favorite and take home a full growler.

1102 Prospect St., 888-632-3379, www.newdaycraft.com

TIP
Check New Day's calendar for special events in the tasting room, such as yoga classes, "mead and knead" chair massages, psychic readings, art exhibitions, and henna tattooing.

THE INDY WINE TRAIL

If you have a designated driver (or an Uber/Lyft account), supplement your visit to New Day Craft with a tour of the four wineries on the Indy Wine Trail. Be sure to try each winery's Traminette, which the Indiana Wine Grape Council has picked as the state's signature wine.

Buck Creek Winery
11747 Indian Creek Rd. South, Indianapolis, 317-862-9463
www.buckcreekwinery.com

Cedar Creek Winery
3820 Leonard Rd., Martinsville, 765-342-9000
www.cedarcreekwine.com

Chateau Thomas Winery
6291 Cambridge Way, Plainfield, 317-837-9463
www.chateauthomas.com

Easley Winery
205 N. College Ave., Indianapolis, 317-636-4516
www.easleywinery.com

Also worth a visit:

Mallow Run Winery
6964 W. Whiteland Rd., Bargersville, 317-422-1556
www.mallowrun.com

Oliver Winery and Vineyards
200 E. Winery Rd., Bloomington, 812-876-5800
www.oliverwinery.com

QUAFF
A CRAFT COCKTAIL

If you've been ordering the same cocktail for years (I see that gin and tonic), it's time to try something new—or perhaps something quite old. Mixologists at Indy's craft cocktail lounges merge pre-Prohibition drink recipes with modern farm-to-table sensibilities, making ingredients in-house and even crafting their own ice cubes. Start at Ball and Biscuit, a sleek, dimly lit lounge named for a 1930s microphone. The cocktails, whose creators are named on the menu, include the Left Me Broker, Drop the Beet, and Smooth Operator. Then head down the street to Tini, a hopping video lounge with cocktails such as the Bodak Swizzle and the Ginnifer Aniseton. In Fountain Square, check out Thunderbird, a former rockabilly hangout that got a revamp in 2014. Opt for a flight of rye whiskey or a cocktail such as the Mr. Big or the Bradshaw. Plan ahead: you're going to need a designated driver.

Ball and Biscuit, 331 Massachusetts Ave., 317-636-0539
www.ballandbiscuit.com

Thunderbird, 1127 Shelby St., 317-974-9580
www.thunderbirdindy.com

Tini, 717 Massachusetts Ave., 317-384-1313
www.tiniontheave.com

BET ON A CREATIVE BRUNCH
AT MILKTOOTH

As the former chef de cuisine at the gone-but-not-forgotten Recess, Jonathan Brooks has some serious culinary street cred. So Indy locals have embraced his "fine diner," Milktooth, a hipster-friendly restaurant that serves "unconventionally creative morning fare" in a renovated garage. When it opened in 2015, it made *Food & Wine*'s list of the best new restaurants in America, and *Condé Nast Traveler* recently named it one of the 207 best restaurants in the *world*. The eatery offers clever twists on classic dishes, such as Dutch baby pancakes and ancient-grains porridge, "of the moment" specials, and side dishes such as sorghum-glazed bacon and pecan sticky buns. Few chefs, in Indy or anywhere, bring such a gourmet sensibility to the humble first meal of the day.

534 Virginia Ave., 317-986-5131
www.milktoothindy.com

INDULGE IN SINFUL CINNAMON TOAST
AT CAFÉ PATACHOU

The original Café Patachou opened in 1989, and even then owner Martha Hoover was sourcing local ingredients and serving farm-to-table cuisine. The locally owned chain now has six locations throughout the city and has been recognized as one of the best restaurants in the nation for breakfast and brunch (although its lunch menu is excellent too). Try the broken-yolk sandwiches and inventive omelets, such as the Overachiever and the Hippie with a Benz. But whatever you order, be sure to get a side of the restaurant's famed cinnamon toast, made with thick-sliced sourdough bread drenched in butter and coated with cinnamon. Yum.

SoBro (the original): 4901 N. Pennsylvania St., 317-925-2823
Downtown: 225 W. Washington St., 317-632-0765
Keystone: 8697 River Crossing Blvd., 317-815-0765
Carmel: 5790 E. Main St., 317-569-0965
Clay Terrace: 14390 Clay Terrace Blvd., 317-566-0765
Indianapolis International Airport: Civic Plaza, 317-241-6224
www.cafepatachou.com

Photo Courtesy of Café Patachou

DON'T WORRY, BE HOPPY
AT INDY'S CRAFT BREWERIES

When Broad Ripple Brewpub opened in 1990, it launched Indy's microbrewery scene with such beers as the Lawn Mower pale ale and the Black Heart lager. Three decades later, our cup runneth over. Indy has more craft breweries than I can count, with new ones opening all the time. Start your brewery tour with the city's top tasting rooms, including Black Acre Brewing, Brugge Brasserie, Flat12 Bierwerks, Fountain Square Brewing Co., Sun King Brewing, Thr3e Wise Men Brewery, Triton Brewing Company, and Upland Brewing Company. Or you can hop on over to HopCat, where many of the bar's 130 taps (the largest draft selection in the state) are dedicated to the city's best brews. In the summer, the Brewers of Indiana Guild's annual Indiana Microbrewers Festival is the perfect overview of Indiana's brewery scene.

TIP

For a guided tour, check out the Indy Brew Bus (www.indybrewbus. com) or try one of the city's multi-passenger party bikes, such as the Handlebar (www.handlebarindy.com), the Pint Cycle (www.thepint-cycle.com), or the Pickled Pedaler (www.thepickledpedaler.com).

Black Acre Brewing
5632 E. Washington St., 317-207-6266
www.blackacrebrewing.com

Broad Ripple Brewpub
842 E. Sixty-Fifth St., 317-253-2739
www.broadripplebrewpub.com

Brugge Brasserie
1011 E. Westfield Blvd., 317-255-0978
www.bruggebrasserie.com

Flat12 Bierwerks
414 N. Dorman St., 317-426-5851
www.flat12.me

Fountain Square Brewing Co.
1301 Barth Ave., 317-493-1410
www.fountainsquarebrewery.com

HopCat
6280 N. College Ave., 317-565-4236
www.hopcat.com/broad-ripple

Sun King Brewing
Multiple locations
www.sunkingbrewing.com

Thr3e Wise Men Brewery
1021 Broad Ripple Ave., 317-255-5151
www.thr3ewisemen.com

Triton Brewing Company
5764 Wheeler Rd., 317-735-2706
www.tritonbrewing.com

Upland Brewing Company
SoBro: 4842 N. College Ave., 317-602-3931
Carmel: 820 E. 116th St., 317-564-3400
www.uplandbeer.com

ORDER AN OLD-SCHOOL DOUGHNUT
AT LONG'S BAKERY

You *could* go to a craft doughnut shop and spend five dollars on a ring of dough with exotic toppings. But it wouldn't be as good as a glazed yeast doughnut from Long's Bakery, which has been serving Indy's sweet tooth since 1955. The simple doughnut is light, fluffy, and melt-in-your-mouth delicious—and here that same five dollars will get you about a dozen yummy treats. Unlike other bakeries that prepare doughnuts in bulk early in the morning, Long's Bakery continues to serve fresh, warm batches all day long. You must come prepared to pay cash and wait in a long line, but you'll soon learn to overlook the inconveniences.

1453 N. Tremont St., 317-632-3741
2301 E. Southport Rd., 317-783-1442

RELISH A CLASSIC REUBEN
AT SHAPIRO'S DELICATESSEN

Founded as a humble grocery store in 1905, Shapiro's Delicatessen is now a regional destination, serving the same corned beef and pastrami as New York City's storied kosher delis. Order the famous Reuben sandwich, made with slow-cooked corned beef, tangy sauerkraut, Swiss cheese, and Thousand Island dressing, sandwiched between hand-cut slices of house-baked rye bread. Or try an old-fashioned favorite, such as smoked tongue, matzo-ball soup, chopped liver, or cabbage borscht. The cafeteria-style restaurant also has a tempting selection of pies, cakes, and cheesecakes, plus breakfast items like bagels and lox.

Downtown (the original): 808 S. Meridian St., 317-631-4041
Keystone: 8702 Keystone Crossing, 317-762-9900
Indianapolis International Airport: 7800 Col. H. Weir Cook Memorial Dr.,
317-241-0645
www.shapiros.com

DEVOUR THE CITY'S BEST SANDWICH:
THE BATALI AT GOOSE THE MARKET

When Chris Eley opened Goose the Market in 2007, he brought craft butchery back to Indianapolis. Now his charcuterie, bacon, and other meaty marvels appear on the menus of every farm-to-fork restaurant in the city. But for the best Goose has to offer, you must go straight to the source. *Bon Appétit* named it one of the ten best sandwich shops in the nation, so head to the deli counter and order a Batali, a sandwich made with spicy coppa, salt-cured capocollo, and soppressata, a dry Italian salami. Toppings include tomato preserves, provolone cheese, hot giardiniera, marinated red onions, mayo, and romaine. Take your sandwich downstairs to the cozy basement *enoteca*, where foodies gather at the communal tables, surrounded by racks of local craft beers and superb wines.

2503 N. Delaware St., 317-924-4944
www.goosethemarket.com

EXTRA CREDIT: THE SMOKING GOOSE MEAT SCHOOL

At the Smoking Goose Meat Locker, Goose's production facility, craft butchers share the tricks of their trade during Smoking Goose Meat School. Learn how to make your own sausage, butcher a whole hog, or truss and cure your own prosciutto. You'll take home plenty of meaty goodies, plus your very own butcher's hat. Just be sure to book early, because these popular classes sell out quickly.

407 N. Dorman St., 317-638-6328
www.smokinggoose.com

WORSHIP
THE SUN KING
AT SUN KING BREWING

The biggest name in Indy brewing is Sun King. In 2015, its rapid growth forced Indiana legislators to increase the legal cap on the number of barrels a microbrewery could produce each year—from thirty thousand to ninety thousand. Its house beers—the Osiris pale ale, Wee Mac Scottish-style ale, and Sunlight cream ale—are available just about everywhere in central Indiana, even in bars that sell mostly Bud Light. But you're better off going straight to the source. At the two tasting rooms, you can order a beer or tasting flight, or refill your Sun King growler (only six dollars on Growler Fill Fridays). To learn more about the brewing process, sign up for a facility tour and hear the incredible story of this local favorite's success.

Downtown: 135 N. College Ave., 317-602-3702
Fishers: 7848 E. Ninety-Sixth St., 317-436-1926
www.sunkingbrewing.com

TIP

Don't bother with the "Legally Required Food Menu" mandated by state law. Although technically you could order the ten-dollar "soup-flavored soup" heated in "the world's most famous microwave," this menu is purely for show.

SEARCH FOR INDY'S
BEST SOUL FOOD

If you're on a quest for comfort food, look no further than the home-style cooking at Indy's best soul food restaurants. The local favorite is Kountry Kitchen Soul Food Place, which serves plates heaped high with meatloaf, smothered pork chops, and crispy fried chicken, all served with fresh-baked cornbread and pitchers of sweet tea.

Maxine's Chicken and Waffles is another top pick. Fried chicken and fluffy waffles are at the top of the menu, of course, but the restaurant also serves such favorites as fried green tomatoes and catfish. The family-owned restaurant uses recipes developed by the family matriarch, Maxine Redmon Bunnell, and it claims to put "a taste of love in every bite." And for sheer bounty, you can't beat Mississippi Belle, a family-style restaurant where platters of fried chicken and slow-roasted pork are refilled (for free!) until you can't eat one more bite.

Kountry Kitchen, 1831 N. College Ave., 317-926-4476
www.kountrykitchenindy.com

Maxine's Chicken and Waffles, 132 N. East St., 317-423-3300
www.maxineschicken.com

Mississippi Belle, 2170 E. Fifty-Fourth St., 317-466-0522

VISIT INDY'S "LITTLE UNITED NATIONS"
FOR ETHNIC DINING IN
LAFAYETTE SQUARE

Once a case study in urban decay, the Lafayette Square neighborhood is now a hot spot for ethnic eats. Dubbed the "little United Nations" by the *New York Times*, its official designation is the International Marketplace. Szechwan Garden is widely regarded as the city's most authentic Chinese restaurant, and Chapati is known for traditional Indian and Pakistani street foods. Try Saigon Restaurant or King Wok for Vietnamese cuisine, Havana Café for Cuban favorites, and Machu Picchu for Peruvian specialties, such as *lomo saltado* and *chicha morada*. Abyssinia serves eat-with-your-fingers Ethiopian cuisine, including an elaborate coffee service. And despite being tucked inside a grocery store, Carniceria Guanajuato is the city's top spot for authentic Mexican food. (Order in Spanish if you can.) Saraga, the city's best international grocery store, is in this neighborhood too.

TIP
Looking for Vietnamese pho? Head to Egg Roll #1 on the city's south side. It looks like a typical pan-Asian takeout joint, but don't be fooled: many locals consider this to be the best pho in the city.

4540 S. Emerson Ave., 317-787-2225, www.eggroll1.com

Abyssinia
5352 W. Thirty-Eighth St., 317-299-0608
www.abyssinianindy.weebly.com

Carniceria Guanajuato
5210 W. Pike Plaza Rd., 317-222-1003
www.carniceriagto.net

Chapati
4930 Lafayette Rd., 317-405-9874
www.eatchapati.com

Havana Café
3839 Moller Rd., 317-293-2822

King Wok
4150 Lafayette Rd., 317-295-8090
www.kingwokindy.com

Machu Picchu
5356 W. Thirty-Eighth St., 317-388-8696

Saigon Restaurant
4760 W. Thirty-Eighth St., 317-927-7270
www.saigonrestaurant-indy.com

Saraga International Grocery
3605 Commercial Dr., 317-388-9999
www.saragafood.com

Szechwan Garden
3649 Lafayette Rd., 317-328-2888
www.szechwangardenindianapolis.com

EXPERIENCE INDY'S
OLD-SCHOOL HANGOUTS

Before Indy had mixology bars and artisan pizzerias, it had dives like Workingman's Friend, which recently celebrated its hundredth birthday. The gritty cash-only pub is known for its smashed burgers, so order a double cheeseburger and a side of onion rings to best appreciate the thin beef patties with crispy edges. Best burger in town? You decide.

Peppy Grill, a hole-in-the-wall diner on the outskirts of Fountain Square, inspires passionate loyalty. The twenty-four-hour greasy spoon serves all-day breakfast, pork tenderloin sandwiches, corned beef hash, burgers, and yummy sour cream potato wedges. Bring some change for the jukebox.

Looking for some 1950s ambiance? The Mug n Bun Drive-In and Indy's Historic Steer-In Restaurant are both known for burgers and breaded pork tenderloin sandwiches. At Mug n Bun, you can pair your sandwich with house-made root beer.

Indy's Historic Steer-In Restaurant, 5130 E. Tenth St., 317-356-0996
www.steerin.net

Mug n Bun Drive-In, 5211 W. Tenth St., 317-244-5669
www.mug-n-bun.com

Peppy Grill, 1004 Virginia Ave., 317-637-1158

Workingman's Friend, 234 N. Belmont Ave., 317-636-2067

FIND YOUR
FAVORITE BURGER

After you've chosen your favorite pork tenderloin sandwich, it's time to move on to burgers. Several new burger joints have opened in Indy in recent years, offering alternatives to the city's old-school hangouts. My favorite is Bru Burger Bar, which tops its juicy "chef burgers" with everything from pear-bacon jam to cucumber sauce. But Punch Burger has a passionate following too. Its offerings include the Texan (grilled onions, cheddar cheese, and barbecue sauce) and the Aloha (ham, grilled pineapple, Swiss cheese, and teriyaki glaze); you can also choose the "build your own burger" option. And in SoBro, check out Twenty Tap, which serves burgers like the French Breakfast and the Angus Khan alongside a stellar selection of craft brews.

Bru Burger Bar, 410 Massachusetts Ave., 317-635-4278
www.bruburgerbar.com

Punch Burger, 137 E. Ohio St., 317-426-5280
www.punchburger.com

Twenty Tap, 5406 N. College Ave., 317-602-8840
www.twentytap.com

EAT MORE,
SPEND LESS

Can't afford to splurge on fine dining? Skip the fast-food chains and try a local option for cheap eats. Start at Yats, which serves Cajun and Creole specialties like jambalaya and chili-cheese étouffée. Entrées cost about six dollars, including rice and garlic bread. Yats now has franchises across the Midwest, but you can't beat the original. And speaking of Indy originals, head to King David Dogs, which opened back in 1941. The restaurant's quarter-pound beef hot dogs, served with inventive toppings like macaroni and cheese, cost less than five dollars. For cheap eats with a Mexican flair, try the Tamale Place, where tamales cost about $3.50. The menu includes spicy options, such as chipotle chicken, and mild options, such as pork in green sauce, as well as vegetarian and dessert tamales.

King David Dogs, 135 N. Pennsylvania St., 317-632-3647
www.kingdaviddogs.com

Tamale Place, 5226 Rockville Rd., 317-248-9771
222 E. Market St., 317-423-2203
1155 E. Stop 11 Rd., 317-300-8748
www.thetamaleplace.com

Yats, ten central Indiana locations
www.yatscajuncreole.com

EAT AN ENTIRE
"BIG UGLY"
AT BUB'S BURGERS AND ICE CREAM

Bub's Burgers and Ice Cream is a family-friendly spot, with two cute locations on the Main Streets of Carmel and Zionsville. But there's a surprise on the standard menu of burgers and fries: the Big Ugly burger, made with a half-pound bun, a full pound of ground beef or elk (*after* cooking), and a pile of toppings. Eat a whole one, bun and all, and your picture goes on the restaurant wall. Eat two, and you get a larger picture. Eat three, and you get a whole poster. Eat four, and the restaurant will display you forever as a life-sized cardboard cutout. Only three people have accomplished that feat: even the Travel Channel's *Man v. Food* host Adam Richman failed. You've got to ask yourself one question: "Do I feel hungry?"

210 W. Main St., Carmel, 317-706-2827
620 S. Main St., Zionsville, 317-344-0927
www.bubsburgersandicecream.com

ENCOUNTER THE RED VELVET ELVIS
AT THE FLYING CUPCAKE BAKERY

The Flying Cupcake was Indy's first cupcake bakery, and it's still easily the best. The shabby-chic bakery's display cases overflow with both regular and filled cupcakes, but you should start with the enormous Red Velvet Elvis. It's made with moist red velvet cake and chocolate chunks, and it's topped with rich cream cheese icing and shavings of white chocolate. Other favorites include the raspberry Razzamatazz, the decadent chocolate ganache, and the bacon-topped Hungry Lumberjack. The bakery also caters to dietary restrictions, offering vegan and gluten-free options at every location but especially at its Illinois Street bakery.

Carmel: 831 S. Rangeline Rd.
Downtown: 423 N. Massachusetts Ave.
Greenwood: 789 US 31 North
Castleton: 4026 E. Eighty-Second St.
SoBro: 5617 N. Illinois St.
Fishers: 13180 Market Square Dr.
317-396-2696
www.theflyingcupcakebakery.com

SATISFY YOUR SWEET TOOTH
WITH INDY'S LOCAL CANDIES

Indy's food scene includes a sweet bunch of confectioners. The most prominent is Endangered Species Chocolate, which supports conservation efforts across the globe. But don't forget the small-scale artisans. My favorite is Newfangled Confections, which creates nutty treats like pralines, spicy candied pecans, and addictive fudge-meets-brittle Frittle candy.

For chocolate lovers, there's Best Chocolate in Town. It's best known for truffles in fun flavors, such as ginger wasabi, cinnamon basil, and gorgonzola (although I'm partial to the salted chocolate caramels and English toffee). Or try Chocolate for the Spirit, especially its award-winning Mayan Spice Bar.

Boutiques like Homespun: Modern Handmade carry local candies alongside gourmet marshmallows from 240sweet and flavored popcorn from Just Pop In. They all make excellent Indy souvenirs, if you can avoid eating them before you get home.

Best Chocolate in Town, 880 Massachusetts Ave., 317-636-2800
www.bestchocolateintown.com
Chocolate for the Spirit, www.chocolateforthespirit.com
Endangered Species Chocolate, www.chocolatebar.com
Newfangled Confections, www.newfangledconfections.com

SCREAM FOR ORGANIC ICE CREAM
AT TRADERS POINT CREAMERY

Tucked away in the woods near Zionsville, Traders Point Creamery is an unexpected surprise. Happy, grass-fed cows produce organic milk, ice cream, yogurt, cheese, and the best cottage cheese you'll ever eat. The farm is open for tours and operates a small store, but the real draw is the charming Loft Restaurant, which is housed in a converted barn. Beneath the exposed wooden beams of the ceiling, you'll dine on farm-to-fork favorites, such as cheese and charcuterie platters, fresh-caught fish, and grass-fed steaks. Don't skip dessert from the Dairy Bar, which serves house-made ice cream in vanilla, chocolate, and seasonal flavors. When your rural retreat is over, you'll be amazed at how quickly you find yourself back in the bustle of the city.

9101 Moore Rd., Zionsville, 317-733-1700
www.traderspointcreamery.com

TAKE A ROAD TRIP
TO FOODIE FINDS IN BLOOMINGTON

Located an hour south of Indianapolis, Bloomington is a college town famous for its culinary sensibilities; *Midwest Living* declared it one of the region's top five food towns. The home of Indiana University has enough offerings to keep foodies busy for weeks, but a good overview begins at FarmBloomington, where chef Daniel Orr puts fresh twists on comfort foods like fried chicken and brisket. Munch on crave-worthy garlic fries as you take in the homey Cracker-Barrel-meets-Anthropologie decor. The city also has a huge array of international eateries, such as the Irish Lion Restaurant and Pub (order the puffballs), the Trojan Horse (Greek), Siam House (Thai), Turkuaz Café (Turkish), and Anyetsang Little Tibet. On the way back to Indy, stop for a tasting at the scenic Oliver Winery, whose versatile Soft Red and Soft White wines are always a bargain.

FarmBloomington, 108 E. Kirkwood Ave., Bloomington, 812-323-0002
www.farm-bloomington.com

Oliver Winery, 200 E. Winery Rd., Bloomington, 812-876-5800
www.oliverwinery.com

VISIT A HOMEGROWN DISTILLERY
AT HOTEL TANGO

When the weather outside is frightful, curl up with a rum-spiked apple cider near the crackling fireplace in Hotel Tango's rustic tasting room. The artisan distillery (not actually a hotel) was founded by Marine veteran Travis Barnes and his wife, Hilary, and its name consists of the owners' initials in the military phonetic alphabet (hotel for Hilary, tango for Travis). The distillery's spirits, including Bravo Bourbon, Golf Gin, Mike Moonshine, Romeo Rum, Victor Vodka, and Whiskey Whiskey, follow the same pattern. While you're here, order a tasting flight or one of the stellar craft cocktails and sneak a peek at the on-site stills.

If you need a snack between drinks, head down the street to one of my favorite restaurants, Rook. It specializes in contemporary Asian street food, such as steamed buns, dumplings, and noodle bowls.

Hotel Tango, 702 Virginia Ave., 317-653-1806
www.hoteltangowhiskey.com

Rook, 501 Virginia Ave., 317-737-2293
www.rookindy.com

BUY A FRESH BREW
AT INDY'S LOCAL COFFEE SHOPS

Yes, there's a Starbucks on every corner, and it's easy to choose convenience over quality. But don't overlook Indy's independent coffee shops, which double as community gathering places. The biggest local chain is Hubbard and Cravens, which has four handy locations; its softly lit Broad Ripple shop is my favorite place to plug in a laptop and get some work done. At Bee Coffee Roasters, baristas take your cup of coffee seriously—even the impromptu artwork in the foam of your latte. Other great options include Coat Check Coffee, the Monon Coffee Company, Calvin Fletcher's Coffee Company, and Kaffeine Coffee—known for special brewing processes that highlight the unique flavors of coffee beans from around the world.

Bee Coffee Roasters
201 S. Capitol Ave., Suite 110, 317-426-2504
5510 Lafayette Rd., Suite 140, 317-280-1236
www.beecoffeeroasters.com

Hubbard and Cravens
Four locations in Indianapolis and Carmel
www.hubbardandcravens.com

Calvin Fletcher's Coffee Company
647 Virginia Ave., 317-423-9697
www.cfcoffeecompany.com

Coat Check Coffee
401 E. Michigan St., 317-550-5008
www.coatcheckcoffee.com

Kaffeine Coffee Company
707 Fulton St., 317-201-4882
www.kaffeinecoffee.com

Monon Coffee Company
920 E. Westfield Blvd., 317-255-0510
www.mononcoffee.com

GIVE IN TO GLUTTONY
AT THE INDIANA STATE FAIR

Forget about counting calories: the Indiana State Fair is the place to splurge on once-a-year treats, such as deep-fried Oreo cookies, sugary lemon shake-ups, and butter-soaked corn on the cob. I always start at the Dairy Bar, where Hoosier dairy farmers serve up grilled-cheese sandwiches and milkshakes. The Indiana Beef Cattle Association offers ribeye sandwiches, and Indiana Pork serves barbecue pulled pork—plus Indiana's signature dish, pork tenderloin sandwiches. Be on the lookout for the latest deep-fried food; past examples have included butter and bubble gum. You can break up the feeding frenzy with the fair's many activities, such as livestock competitions, concerts, and a midway full of rides and carnival games. As Rodgers and Hammerstein wrote, "Our state fair is a great state fair. Don't miss it. Don't even be late."

1202 E. Thirty-Eighth St., 317-927-7500
www.in.gov/statefair/fair

Photo Courtesy of Chris-Crawl and Dance Kaleidoscope

MUSIC AND ENTERTAINMENT

GET AN INDY ARTS OVERVIEW
AT SPOTLIGHT

Spotlight is an annual fund-raiser for the Indiana AIDS Fund, and it brings together just about every performing arts group in central Indiana. So it's a perfect opportunity to get an overview of Indy's artistic assets. Held at Clowes Hall on the campus of Butler University, Spotlight features mini-performances from choral ensembles, musical groups, dance troupes, theater companies, spoken-word poets, and even drag queens. Sometimes groups preview upcoming performances, and sometimes they offer something completely new; you never know what to expect next. Best of all, Spotlight has raised more than ten million dollars over the years for HIV/AIDS testing and treatment.

www.spotlightindy.org

RSVP TO INDY'S HIPPEST PARTY:
TONIC BALL

Since 2002, Tonic Ball has served as an annual fund-raiser for Second Helpings, a nonprofit organization that gathers unused food from restaurants and grocery stores and uses it to prepare meals for people in need. But this is no formal black-tie affair. Each November, organizers pick iconic bands, such as the Beatles, Fleetwood Mac, or Nirvana, and ask local musicians to cover their songs. Originally held at Radio Radio in Fountain Square, the fund-raiser has since expanded to four other nearby venues. So basically it's a giant Fountain Square block party, complete with an art gallery and a silent auction. And everyone knows it, so buy your tickets the instant they go on sale.

www.tonicindy.com

HEAR THE MIDWEST'S BEST BLUES
AT THE SLIPPERY NOODLE

Founded in 1850, the Slippery Noodle is Indiana's oldest bar and oldest surviving commercial building. In its early years, the Noodle served as a way station on the Underground Railroad. (That's why there's a ghost in the basement.) During Prohibition, the owners made bootleg alcohol in the basement, and John Dillinger's gang used the stable for target practice. These days, however, the Noodle is one of the best venues in the Midwest for live blues. Come on Wednesdays for the popular open-stage blues jam, or stop by on weekends to see such bands as the Why Store, the Warrior Kings, the Gordon Bonham Blues Band, and the Gene Deer Band. The bar has two stages, so you'll often get two shows for the price of one cover charge.

372 S. Meridian St., 317-631-6974
www.slipperynoodle.com

LIGHT UP YOUR LIFE
AT WINTERLIGHTS

In 2017, the Indianapolis Museum of Art developed a new holiday event, Winterlights, by stringing up more than a million lights in stunning, artistic displays throughout its park-like grounds (recently rebranded as Newfields). The museum expected to sell thirty-five thousand tickets, but actual attendance was closer to seventy thousand—so, not surprisingly, Winterlights is now an annual event. The first season's highlight was the Landscape of Light, a sprawling lawn of light displays choreographed to music from *The Nutcracker*. (I watched the whole show four times.) When you need to warm up, find the nearest bonfire or buy a hot chocolate or apple cider—spiked if you wish—from the kiosks. Winterlights also includes a peek into the Lilly House while it is lavishly decorated for the holidays. Here's to the most wonderful time of the year—and to new traditions.

4000 Michigan Rd., 317-923-1331
www.discovernewfields.org

BANG THE DRUM ALL DAY
AT THE RHYTHM! DISCOVERY CENTER

Many locals still don't know about the Rhythm! Discovery Center, which opened downtown in 2009. The percussion museum, which is managed by the Percussive Arts Society, displays rare percussion artifacts, from ancient instruments to modern rock-and-roll drum sets. But what you really want to know is, can I make some noise? Yes, you can. You can bang a giant gong, learning about the properties of sound at the same time. Then you can join the drum circle or play hundreds of different instruments in the interactive gallery. You can even head into a soundproof booth to crash cymbals and bang on drum kits to your heart's content. As long as you're having fun, you won't notice how badly you need earplugs.

110 W. Washington St., 317-275-9030
www.rhythmdiscoverycenter.org

SHARE SOME LAUGHS
AT INDY'S BEST COMEDY CLUBS

If you liked *Whose Line Is It Anyway,* you'll love ComedySportz. Each night the improv comedy group splits into teams—the win goes to the team that gets the most laughs. The late-night Blue Show can get downright raunchy, but most other shows are family friendly. And if you catch the improv bug, ComedySportz also offers improv classes for both kids and adults.

Indy has traditional comedy clubs too, including Morty's Comedy Joint and Crackers Comedy Club. The two clubs compete for the same headlining performers, who might soon appear on *Last Comic Standing* or even snag their own sitcoms. Crackers has a shiny new venue downtown—convenient for dinner beforehand or clubbing afterward. Morty's, on the north side, has a wider food selection, making it a better choice for an all-in-one outing.

ComedySportz, 721 Massachusetts Ave., 317-951-8499
www.indycomedysportz.com

Crackers, 207 N. Delaware, 317-631-3536
www.crackerscomedy.com

Morty's Comedy Joint, 3824 E. Eighty-Second St., 317-848-5500
www.mortyscomedy.com

PARTY LIKE A PENGUIN
AT ZOOBILATION

At Zoobilation, the Indianapolis Zoo's annual black-tie fund-raiser, the penguins aren't the only ones wearing tuxedos. Despite the summer heat, thousands of people roam the grounds in suits and animal-themed evening gowns, sipping free top-shelf cocktails and nibbling samples from seventy of the city's best restaurants. (For local chefs, the Zoobilation People's Choice Award is a highly coveted prize.) Multiple bands perform throughout the grounds, a DJ creates a pop-up dance party, and the zoo's nocturnal animals make appearances that daytime visitors never get to see. Tickets are a whopping three hundred dollars each, but no one seems to mind—they sell out in mere minutes. And it's money well spent: the Indianapolis Zoo is the nation's largest privately funded zoo, and each year Zoobilation supports its mission by raising more than two million dollars in a single night.

1200 W. Washington St., 317-630-2001
www.indyzoo.com

GET TUNED UP
AT INDY'S JAZZ CLUBS

The Slippery Noodle's stellar blues lineup may get all the press, but jazz fans in Indy have some great options too, including the Chatterbox on Mass Ave and the Jazz Kitchen in SoBro. Both have been around for decades, and both offer a mix of big-name performances and casual jam sessions. The Jazz Kitchen is a larger, more upscale venue, with a full menu of dishes inspired by Cajun and Creole cuisine. But the cozy little Chatterbox makes for intimate performances, and it's worth a stop just to read the extensive bathroom graffiti. The Chatterbox menu is extremely limited, but it balances the scales by serving delicious meat pies from Patties of Jamaica—one of Indy's best-kept foodie secrets. If you have to choose just one, it's a toss-up, so check the performance calendars to see which lineup appeals to you more.

Chatterbox, 435 Massachusetts Ave., 317-636-0584
www.chatterboxjazz.com

Jazz Kitchen, 5377 N. College Ave., 317-253-4900
www.thejazzkitchen.com

FIND YOUR POLKA GROOVE
AT THE RATHSKELLER

The Rathskeller opened its doors in 1894 inside the Athenaeum, a social club for German immigrants. Now it's the city's oldest restaurant, and it still celebrates its Deutschland roots. It serves a hearty beer list and all the foods you'd find in a Munich beer hall: bratwurst, sauerbraten, schnitzel, and sauerkraut. But the best part is the outdoor biergarten, which is one of the city's best outdoor venues for live music. If you see just one band here, it should be Polka Boy. The local favorite adds a polka twist to classic tunes such as "My Sharona," "Folsom Prison Blues," and even "The Star-Spangled Banner."

401 E. Michigan St., 317-636-0396
www.rathskeller.com

PUNCH UP YOUR NIGHT OUT
AT PUNCH BOWL SOCIAL

Imagine getting your friends together and visiting a bowling alley, a vintage arcade, a karaoke bar, a pool hall, a restaurant, and a cocktail bar—all in one evening. Sure, it would be an epic night out, but can you imagine the Uber tab? Punch Bowl Social offers all these things in one place, plus table games such as ping-pong, foosball, and air hockey. The full restaurant menu is served all day, along with plenty of extras, including fresh juices, spiked milkshakes, and—of course—massive bowls of boozy punch. And the karaoke rooms are private, so only your friends will see your drunken rendition of "MMMBop," unless the video winds up on YouTube.

120 S. Meridian St., 317-249-8613
www.punchbowlsocial.com/location/indianapolis

SEE THE BEST OF MODERN DANCE
AT DANCE KALEIDOSCOPE

If you enjoy TV shows like *So You Think You Can Dance*, you'll love Dance Kaleidoscope. It's the state's oldest professional dance company specializing in contemporary dance, and it consistently brings new ideas to the stage. The troupe performs at the Indiana Repertory Theatre, and its musical selections range from classical music and jazz standards to Broadway favorites and recent pop hits. Dance Kaleidoscope also appears at community arts festivals; every year it offers up one of my favorite performances at the IndyFringe theater festival. One year its choreography, set to Tchaikovsky's *Romeo and Juliet*, actually left me in tears, and not just because I'm a Shakespeare geek.

317-940-6555
www.dancekal.org

PICNIC WITH MOZART
AT SYMPHONY ON THE PRAIRIE

For most of the year, the Indianapolis Symphony Orchestra performs in the Hilbert Circle Theatre on Monument Circle. But in the summer, the city's most talented classical musicians head north to the suburb of Fishers, where they perform in an outdoor amphitheater at Conner Prairie. Set against a beautiful backdrop of sunsets and starry nights, the Symphony on the Prairie series highlights a wide range of music, from Beethoven symphonies to Beatles hits. All you need is a picnic basket and a bottle of wine.

13400 Allisonville Rd., Fishers, 317-639-4300
www.indianapolissymphony.org

TIP
Symphony on the Prairie's Independence Day concerts are top sellers, so buy tickets for those performances as soon as possible, and plan to arrive early to snag the best spots on the lawn.

CELEBRATE WITH SACRED MUSIC
AT CHRIST CHURCH CATHEDRAL

In Europe, tourists crowd the great cathedrals to hear choral performances and organ recitals. In Indianapolis, Monument Circle's Christ Church Cathedral offers a similar experience, albeit on a much smaller scale. The Episcopal church has three choirs. Founded in 1883, the Choir of Men and Choristers is the oldest of the three groups, and it has recorded several albums and toured the globe. Coro Latinoamericano was founded in 2000, and the Gallery Choir—a casual, mixed-voice group for people who love to sing—was established in 2016. Despite its small size, the church also has three organs. Check the church calendar for upcoming choral concerts and organ recitals, or simply unwind after work with an evensong service (Thursdays at 5:15 p.m.).

125 Monument Circle, 317-636-4577
www.cccindy.org

TIP

Christ Church's main fund-raiser is the one-day Strawberry Festival, held each June on Monument Circle. Downtown workers leave their offices in droves to stand in line for strawberry shortcake, the festival's signature treat (cash only).

SEEK OUT THAT OLD-FASHIONED SWING:
THE CABARET

The Cabaret revives a bygone era, pairing elegant dinner service with intimate vocal performances from well-known stars. The club got its start in borrowed venues, including the swanky Columbia Club, but it recently opened a venue of its own. Past performers have included Megan Mullally, Alan Cumming, Nellie McKay, Jane Lynch, and Leslie Odom Jr. Craft cocktails and a new, expanded menu—fittingly designed by the culinary team at the Jazz Kitchen—combine with the music for a perfect night out. As the song from the musical *Cabaret* says, "What good is sitting alone in your room? Come hear the music play."

924 N. Pennsylvania St., Suite B, 317-275-1169
www.thecabaret.org

VISIT CARMEL'S STUNNING CONCERT HALL:
THE PALLADIUM AT THE CENTER FOR THE PERFORMING ARTS

If the Palladium reminds you of a European opera house, you're not alone. The concert hall is beautiful inside and out, and the acoustics are absolute perfection. It's the centerpiece of the Center for the Performing Arts, which is in turn the centerpiece of Carmel's massive City Center development. Under the artistic direction of Grammy-nominated crooner Michael Feinstein, the Palladium draws performers such as Dennis Miller, Itzhak Perlman, Tony Bennett, Trisha Yearwood, Kenny Rogers, and "Weird Al" Yankovic. The audience skews a bit older than other local music venues, but that doesn't mean you need to rent a tuxedo or commission a couture gown; the Palladium prides itself on its casual vibe. On the other hand, thanks to a local car dealership's sponsorship of the valet service, you do get free valet parking if you show up in a Jaguar.

1 Center Green, Carmel, 317-843-3800
www.thecenterfortheperformingarts.com

GO DOWN THE RABBIT HOLE
AT THE WHITE RABBIT CABARET

For sheer weirdness, it's hard to beat the performance lineup at the White Rabbit Cabaret. The Fountain Square venue presents some things you might expect: live music, dance parties, stand-up comedy, and trivia nights. But it also schedules fake spelling bees, fake author talks, and screenings of films of dubious quality (for example, *Space Jam* and *What About Bob*). Regular events include Lloyd and Harvey's Wowie Zowie Show, featuring variety acts both good and bad; the Burlesque Bingo Bango Show, a bingo game with truly ridiculous prizes; and the oddball Let's Make a Date Gameshow, which has been running for five years. White Rabbit is also the home of Rocket Doll Revue, Indy's premier burlesque troupe. Its shows are a body-positive delight—more irreverent than salacious—and are perfect for a raucous girls' night out.

1116 Prospect St., 317-686-9550
www.whiterabbitcabaret.com

SPORTS AND RECREATION

EXPERIENCE
INDIANA BASKETBALL

The old saying is true: in forty-nine states it's just basketball, but this is Indiana. If you count how many homes have basketball hoops in the driveway, you'll begin to understand the intensity of Hoosiers' passion. To deepen that understanding, you have to watch *Hoosiers.* It's a true Cinderella story about a high school team from tiny Milan, Indiana, and it fueled vehement opposition to the state athletic association's move, more than twenty years ago, to separate teams into classes based on school size—still a hugely controversial decision.

Now you're ready for some games. Indy is home to the NBA's Indiana Pacers and the WNBA's Indiana Fever, both of which play at Bankers Life Fieldhouse. College hoops get you closer to the action, so watch the Butler University Bulldogs play at Indy's historic Hinkle Fieldhouse. And, as *Hoosiers* suggests, high school is the true heart of Hoosier basketball, so pick a Friday night and go cheer for your neighborhood team.

Butler University Bulldogs: www.butlersports.com
Indiana Fever: www.wnba.com/fever
Indiana Pacers: www.nba.com/pacers

RUN THE RACETRACK
AT THE MINI-MARATHON

Each May, the 500 Festival kicks off its month-long celebration with the Mini-Marathon, one of the nation's largest half marathons. Even with thirty-five thousand slots, it often sells out months in advance. What's the appeal? Perhaps it's that the route includes a 2.5-mile loop around the Indianapolis Motor Speedway—which practically counts as hallowed ground in Indianapolis. The Mini-Marathon also comes at just the right time to serve as a motivational goal for runners who start training because of New Year's resolutions. Can't handle 13.1 miles? Neither can I. Fortunately, there's a 5K option as well.

www.500festival.com/mini-marathon

GO TO A COLTS GAME
AT LUCAS OIL STADIUM

Indiana is basketball territory, but Indy residents love their football team too. The NFL's Indianapolis Colts play at Lucas Oil Stadium, which opened in 2008 to replace the antiquated RCA Dome. The stadium seats sixty-seven thousand fans and offers a great view of the downtown skyline, so seeing a football game here is an essential Indy experience, even if you're not much of a sports fan.

Can't make it to a game? Sign up instead for a behind-the-scenes stadium tour, which includes visits to the playing field, locker room, and press box. The usual tour schedule is 11 a.m., 1 p.m., and 3 p.m., Monday through Friday.

500 S. Capitol Ave., 317-262-8600
www.lucasoilstadium.com

FUN FACT
Each of the two panels in Lucas Oil Stadium's retractable roof weighs 2.5 million pounds.

SHAKE UP
YOUR FITNESS ROUTINE

Indy has a plethora of fitness opportunities, from indoor gyms to outdoor trails. But even hardcore fitness buffs can get stuck in a rut, making exercise feel like a chore. Fortunately, both Sky Zone and CirqueIndy offer ways to break up the routine. At Sky Zone, an indoor trampoline park in Fishers, you can jump into SkyFit classes; the bouncy aerobic workout burns up to a thousand calories an hour. Or try CirqueIndy, where you can strengthen your muscles by suspending yourself with aerial silks and hoops. The traveling circus is unfortunately a thing of the past, so this is the closest you'll ever get to running away and joining the circus.

CirqueIndy, 617 N. Fulton St., 317-758-7455
www.cirqueindy.com

Sky Zone, 10080 E. 121st St., Fishers, 317-572-2999
www.skyzone.com/fishers

SEE BASEBALL
UP CLOSE
WITH THE INDIANAPOLIS INDIANS

You can root, root, root for the home team at Victory Field, where cheering for the minor-league Indianapolis Indians is like stepping back in time. The tickets are affordable, the stadium is small, and the concession stands still serve peanuts and Cracker Jack.

Victory Field is part of downtown's White River State Park, and it offers a spectacular view of the city skyline—especially in the summer, when games on Friday evenings are followed by a free fireworks show. No wonder *Sports Illustrated* dubbed it "the best minor-league ballpark in the nation."

Looking for a bargain? Sign up the kiddos for the Knot Hole Kids Club. Membership includes discounted tickets and a chance to run the bases after Sunday home games.

501 W. Maryland St., 317-269-3545
www.indyindians.com

GO PADDLING
AT EAGLE CREEK PARK

Eagle Creek Park is the largest park in the city and one of the largest city parks in the nation. Its amenities include a beach and marina, a pistol range, several nature centers, hiking trails, and the GoApe Treetop Adventure park. The park's Eagle Creek Outfitters rents out canoes, stand-up paddleboards, kayaks, pontoon boats, and sailboats. But don't overlook its guided paddle programs, where you'll kayak or canoe with a tour guide and hear interesting stories about the park and its animal inhabitants. Book early for nighttime tours, which are offered only when the moon is full; sunset paddle tours are popular too.

7840 W. Fifty-Sixth St., 317-327-7110
www.indy.gov/eaglecreek

CLIMB A TREE
AT GoApe TREETOP ADVENTURE

Located within Eagle Creek Park, the GoApe Treetop Adventure is a physically challenging aerial obstacle course, complete with zip lines, rope ladders, suspension bridges, balance challenges, and Tarzan-style rope swings. The course has five sections, with thirty-nine crossings and a total length of nearly half a mile. The highest point of the course is forty-one feet, so GoApe isn't for those who are terrified of heights (except, perhaps, as a form of immersion therapy), and there are also some restrictions on weight, height, and age. For most people, though, the GoApe Treetop Adventure is a fun outdoor activity with a unique reward—a bird's-eye view of one of the prettiest parks in the city.

5855 Delong Rd., 800-971-8271
www.goape.com

GO GREEN
AT INDY'S GOLF COURSES

Famed golf-course architect Pete Dye is from Indiana, so it makes sense that he designed more golf courses here than in any other state. The most iconic is Brickyard Crossing, which is next to the Indianapolis Motor Speedway; four of the course's holes are located in the speedway's infield. The Pete Dye Golf Trail highlights seven of the architect's courses, which include the Eagle Creek Golf Club at Eagle Creek Park and the Fort Golf Course at Fort Harrison State Park. Dye's "first great golf course," the one that made him a star, is Crooked Stick Golf Club in Carmel. Alas, you can't walk those links without an invitation from a member.

For a challenging course not designed by Dye, tee up at Noblesville's Purgatory Golf Club. Watch out for the tricky seventeenth hole; its abundant sand traps have earned it the nickname "hell's half-acre."

Brickyard Crossing, 4400 W. Sixteenth St., 317-492-6417
www.brickyardcrossing.com

Crooked Stick Golf Club, 1964 Burning Tree Lane, Carmel, 317-844-9938
www.crookedstick.org

Pete Dye Golf Trail
www.petedyegolftrail.com

Purgatory Golf Club, 12160 E. 216th St., Noblesville, 317-776-4653
www.purgatorygolf.com

EXPLORE INDY BY BIKE
ON THE INDIANAPOLIS CULTURAL TRAIL

There's nothing in the world quite like the Indianapolis Cultural Trail. The eight-mile cycling and pedestrian path connects six of the city's downtown cultural districts, including Fountain Square, White River State Park, and Mass Ave. It links to the Broad Ripple district via the Monon Trail, a busy urban greenway stretching ten miles from downtown Indy to Carmel. No bike? No problem. The city's bike-share program has twenty-five rental stations across the city, and you can purchase either a day pass or an annual membership. Indianapolis may be known for its auto racing, but slowly it's becoming a city you can explore without a car.

www.indyculturaltrail.org

EXPERIENCE THE GREATEST SPECTACLE IN RACING:
THE INDIANAPOLIS 500

Without seeing the Indianapolis Motor Speedway in person, it's hard to comprehend the scale of the world's largest venue for spectator sports. Constructed in 1909, the facility encloses a 2.5-mile oval track and can seat a quarter of a million race fans.

Since 1911, the speedway's signature event has been the Indianapolis 500, where thirty-three of the world's top IndyCar drivers compete at speeds of up to 237 miles per hour. Held annually on the Sunday before Memorial Day, the "greatest spectacle in racing" is steeped in tradition, such as singing "Back Home Again in Indiana" before the race and watching the winner quench his—and someday her—thirst with a glass bottle of milk.

4790 W. Sixteenth St., 317-492-8500
www.indianapolismotorspeedway.com

INSIDER TIP

Book a seat in turn one, where you'll have the best view of the finish line, the pits, and all the risky racing action. And bring a radio scanner, which lets you eavesdrop on the drivers and their pit crews.

GO BEYOND
THE FINISH LINE

The Indianapolis 500 happens just once a year, but Indy celebrates its racing culture year-round. To explore the history of the race, head to the Indianapolis Motor Speedway Museum on the speedway grounds. It displays a century's worth of racecars, with exhibits describing advances in safety and speed. Look for the Marmon Wasp, which Ray Harroun drove to victory at the inaugural Indy 500 in 1911.

Just down the street is the Dallara IndyCar Factory, where you can see IndyCar production up close or hop inside a racing simulator. Need an even bigger adrenaline fix? Check out Indy Racing Experience. For a steep fee, you can drive an actual racecar around the track. You get just three laps, but you'll reach speeds up to 130 miles per hour.

Indianapolis Motor Speedway Museum
4790 W. Sixteenth St., 317-492-6784
www.indyracingmuseum.org

Dallara IndyCar Factory and Indy Racing Experience
1201 Main St., Speedway, 317-243-7171
www.indycarfactory.com
www.indyracingexperience.com

STOP AND SMELL THE ROSES
AT INDY'S PRETTIEST GARDENS

When you need respite from the hustle and bustle, seek refuge in one of the city's beautiful gardens. On the south side of town, the ten-thousand-square-foot Garfield Park Conservatory offers a year-round display of tropical plants, and the park's Sunken Garden mimics the formal gardens of Europe. Downtown, the Indianapolis Zoo's White River Gardens is a three-acre botanical garden best known for its spring tulips. Each summer, White River Gardens fills its five-thousand-square-foot conservatory with thousands of butterflies, including rare species from across the globe. On the north side, Butler University's campus is home to Holcomb Gardens, a twenty-acre swath of woodlands and formal gardens. Bring a picnic blanket and sprawl near the statue of Persephone, the Greek goddess whose annual return from the underworld heralds the arrival of spring.

Garfield Park Conservatory and Sunken Garden
2505 Conservatory Dr., 317-327-7184
www.garfieldgardensconservatory.org

Holcomb Gardens, 4600 Sunset Ave., 800-368-6852
www.butler.edu

White River Gardens, 1200 W. Washington St., 317-630-2001
www.indianapoliszoo.com

TAKE A ROAD TRIP
TO INDIANA'S OUTDOOR GETAWAYS

The gem of Indiana's state park system is Brown County State Park, located about an hour south of Indianapolis. The sixteen-thousand-acre park is best known for its fall foliage, but its extensive trail system offers scenic vistas year-round of southern Indiana's rolling hills. Not far away, the Hoosier National Forest stretches for 202,000 acres, offering more than 260 miles of trails for hiking, mountain biking, and horseback riding. Both parks are prime spots for overnight camping trips; if you're not a camper, consider booking a room at Brown County State Park's cozy Abe Martin Lodge.

Southern Indiana is also home to the Hilly Hundred, one of the state's most popular long-distance cycling tours. The three-day event is held each October to give cyclists an up-close view of the foliage.

Brown County State Park, 1810 State Rd. 46 E., Nashville
812-988-6406
www.in.gov/dnr/parklake/2988.htm

Hilly Hundred
www.hillyhundred.org

Hoosier National Forest, 811 Constitution Ave., Bedford
812-275-5987
www.fs.usda.gov/hoosier

CHEER ON THE LEAD JAMMER
WITH NAPTOWN ROLLER DERBY

Even if you're not a sports fan, you'll have a blast with the Naptown Roller Derby team, part of the Women's Flat Track Derby Association. Indy's edgiest sports team includes skaters such as Amelia B. Killya, Crash N2U, Trudy Bauchery, Mutant Jean, and Vivi Section, who shove and elbow their way to victory on the oval track. Join the raucous crowd in the stands at the Indiana State Fairgrounds Coliseum, or come early to snag a coveted "suicide seat" (adults only) on the floor at the edge of the track. You may get kicked in the face with a roller skate, but you'll have the best view of the fast-paced frenzy.

Want to get in on the action? Sign up for a Naptown Roller Derby workshop. The Calm before the Storm series is Derby 101. In the Storm Chasers series, participants start to build serious skating skills. If you fall in love with roller derby, you may soon need a wacky name of your own.

www.naptownrollerderby.com

BE A PINHEAD
AT DUCKPIN BOWLING IN FOUNTAIN SQUARE

Duckpin bowling is primarily an East Coast pastime, and it reached its peak of popularity way back in the 1920s. So Fountain Square Theatre is the only place in the Midwest to try this scaled-back version of bowling, which utilizes smaller pins and grapefruit-sized balls. Scoring works the same way, but in duckpin bowling you get three balls per turn instead of two. The Fountain Square Theatre building has eight lanes on the fourth floor and seven lanes in the basement. Both rooms have a vintage feel, complete with jukeboxes and bowling memorabilia.

1105 Prospect St., 317-686-6006
www.fountainsquareindy.com/action-atomic-duckpin-bowling

INSIDER TIP
Reservations are essential, especially on weekends.

JOIN THE SOCCER CRAZE
WITH THE INDY ELEVEN

My late father-in-law used to joke that soccer was the sport of the future and always would be. Fans of the Indy Eleven would beg to differ. Indy's professional soccer team was founded in 2013 and rapidly built its fan base, becoming the first team in the history of the North American Soccer League to sell out every home game of its inaugural season. At first, the Indy Eleven played its home games at the IU Michael A. Carroll Track and Soccer Stadium, but it has since graduated to Lucas Oil Stadium—and has big plans for its very own venue. Tickets start at an affordable fifteen dollars, so come see the sport of the future, today.

www.indyeleven.com

WALK THE CANAL
AT WHITE RIVER STATE PARK

For the prettiest stroll in Indy, head to the Canal Walk, which winds 1.5 miles from White River State Park to Eleventh Street. Along the way, you'll see a range of public art, including several murals. My favorite is Kyle Ragsdale's *Hoosier Hospitality on the Boatload of Knowledge*, which depicts an attempt to create a utopian community in tiny New Harmony, Indiana. If you get tired of walking, head to the park's Wheel Fun Rentals, which rents surreys, pedal cars, and bicycles, as well as kayaks and pedal boats. Nearby, Old World Gondoliers offers gondola rides just like the ones in Venice, complete with striped shirts and serenades. While you're in the area, you can explore Indy's museum campus, visit the Indianapolis Zoo, or take a walking tour of Indy's many war memorials.

www.canalwalkindy.com

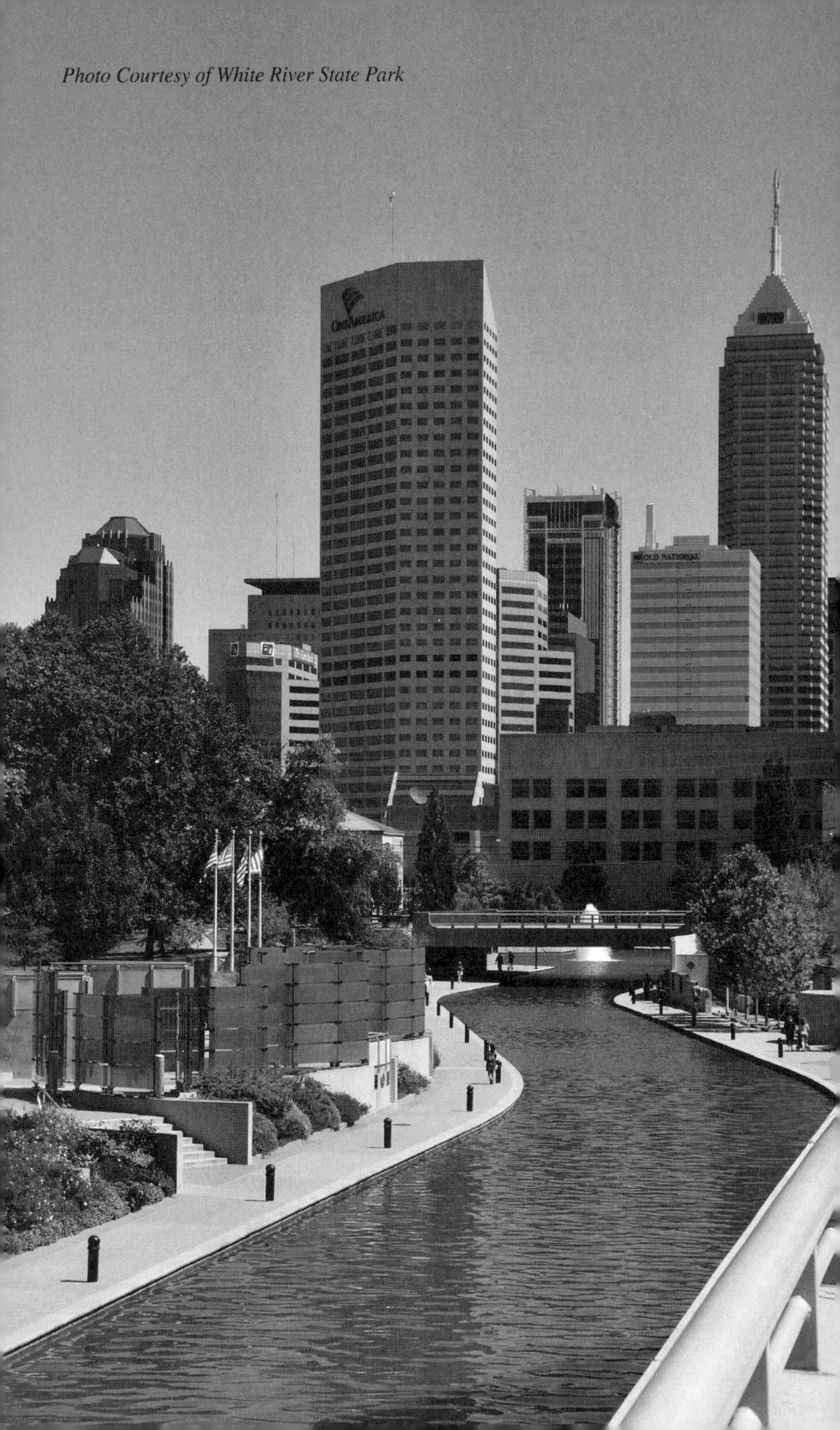

Photo Courtesy of White River State Park

TAKE A ROAD TRIP
TO INDIANA'S BECOMING AN OUTDOORSWOMAN CAMP

Do you know how to shoot a compound bow? Survive alone in the forest? Sew a coonskin cap? Identify edible plants in the wild? If not, head to Becoming an Outdoorswoman, an annual ladies-only retreat organized by the Indiana Department of Natural Resources. Held each May at Ross Camp in West Lafayette, the weekend workshop demystifies outdoor survival skills, from basics like backpacking and campfire cooking to advanced skills like trapping wild game and shooting muzzleloaders. The weekend culminates in a survival challenge to see which team has best mastered skills like starting fires, shooting clay pigeons, and identifying animal footprints. Just remember to come prepared for basic bunkhouse accommodations; an air mattress is highly recommended.

www.indianabow.com

FALL HARD FOR CURLING
WITH THE CIRCLE CITY CURLING CLUB

Watching curling during the Winter Olympics can be bewildering: Why, for example, are people sweeping the ice with brooms? What's all this talk about "ends" and "stones"? You'll get answers—and hands-on experience—at the Circle City Curling Club's Learn to Curl clinics. Each session includes twenty minutes of classroom time, where you'll hear about the rules and safety procedures (including how to fall correctly). Then, out on the ice, you'll learn how to launch stones, sweep, score, and strategize, and you'll put those skills to use in a mini-match with other beginners. Trust me, it's harder than it looks on TV, but don't worry about looking foolish. Yes, you will fall—but so will everyone else. And if you fall in love with curling, the club has leagues for players of all skill levels.

www.circlecitycurling.wordpress.com

INSIDER TIP

The Learn to Curl clinics always sell out quickly—it took me several years to snag a slot. When you see new clinic dates posted online, submit your registration right away.

CULTURE AND HISTORY

SIGHTSEE ON MONUMENT CIRCLE
WITH INDIANA LANDMARKS WALKING TOURS

Indy's centerpiece is the towering neoclassical Soldiers and Sailors Monument, dedicated in 1902 to honor the city's war veterans. The bronze *Victory* statue atop the limestone obelisk faces south, toward Union Station, to welcome Indy's soldiers back home. Surrounding it is Monument Circle, which gives Indy its Circle City nickname. The monument's observation deck offers stunning views of the city, and Indiana Landmarks enriches the experience with informative walking tours. Guides describe Alexander Ralston's original plan for the city's layout and discuss the surrounding architecture. One thing you won't see on the Circle is the original governor's residence, which was torn down in 1857; the new residence is farther north, on swanky Meridian Street.

317-639-4534
www.indianalandmarks.org

FOUR MORE
REASONS TO VISIT
MONUMENT CIRCLE

1. The annual Circle of Lights tree-lighting ceremony, which transforms the Soldiers and Sailors Monument into the world's tallest Christmas tree.

2. The annual Strawberry Festival, at which Christ Church Cathedral dishes up six tons of strawberries and more than eighteen thousand homemade shortcakes.

3. The Indianapolis Symphony Orchestra, which performs at Monument Circle's historic Hilbert Circle Theatre.

4. Moving organ and choral concerts at Christ Church Cathedral.

RIDE A HISTORIC CAROUSEL
AT THE CHILDREN'S MUSEUM
OF INDIANAPOLIS

The world's largest children's museum is a wonderland of dinosaurs, trains, mummies, carnival rides, and much more. In the Dinosphere exhibit, an immersive IMAX environment brings to life the sounds, smells, and sights of the dinosaur era. In ScienceWorks, kids can race boats down an indoor creek and climb aboard construction equipment. In Treasures of the Earth, visitors can reconstruct an Egyptian mummy or a Chinese terra-cotta warrior. The museum also has a planetarium, a huge play area for babies and toddlers, and a stunning five-story glass sculpture by artist Dale Chihuly.

But the best spot by far is the Carousel Wishes and Dreams exhibit, which is home to a restored 1917 carousel you can actually ride. The exhibit also has funhouse mirrors and mazes, a treehouse, and vintage video games. You'll only get the kids to leave by promising them a visit to the enormous gift shop on the way out.

3000 N. Meridian St., 317-334-4000
www.childrensmuseum.org

SEEK OUT INDY'S SPOOKY SIDE
WITH IRVINGTON GHOST TOURS

Located five miles east of downtown Indy, Irvington was the city's first upscale suburb. Although the neighborhood was annexed back in 1902, its residents maintain a fierce sense of community pride. Looking for a fun way to explore the neighborhood's winding streets and Victorian architecture? Your best bet is Irvington Ghost Tours, which offers two-hour walking tours (cash only) throughout October in conjunction with the neighborhood's fabulous Halloween festival. Volunteer guides share stories about John Dillinger, who robbed an Irvington drugstore before he robbed his first bank, and serial killer H. H. Holmes, of *Devil in the White City* fame.

But the ghost you should remember is Madge Oberholtzer. In 1925, the bright young teacher was kidnapped, tortured, and murdered by D. C. Stephenson, the grand dragon of the state's Ku Klux Klan. Her deathbed statement led to Stephenson's conviction and permanently crippled the KKK's hold on Indiana politics. Both of their homes are included on the tour.

6 S. Johnson Ave., 317-850-1910
www.indianaghosttours.org

CHECK IN
AT THE INDIANAPOLIS MUSEUM OF CONTEMPORARY ART

The Indianapolis Museum of Contemporary Art doesn't have a permanent collection, so it constantly refreshes the Indy arts scene with its temporary exhibitions. You never know what's coming next. Stop by for architectural retrospectives, surrealist films, found-object sculptures, and even interactive paint-by-numbers wall murals. IMOCA's gallery is within the Hotel Alexander, which has its own share of noteworthy local art. Try to stop by on First Fridays, when Indy's art galleries stay open late to showcase their latest exhibitions. And stay tuned for information about a new iMOCA venue coming soon.

216 E. South St.
317-790-5757
www.indymoca.org

WATCH
THE PARADE PASS BY

Each May, three hundred thousand spectators line Indy's downtown streets for the 500 Festival Parade, part of the month-long celebration of the Indianapolis 500. Splurge on a reserved seat in the bleachers to see racecar drivers, marching bands, fancy floats, and giant balloons. Next up on Indy's parade schedule is June's Circle City IN Pride Festival, Indiana's largest LGBT celebration. Its signature event, the Cadillac Barbie Pride Parade, is named for the drag queen who founded the festival. Finally, mark your calendar for the Circle City Classic Parade, held each October in conjunction with the Circle City Classic—a football game featuring teams from two historically black colleges or universities. It's part of Indiana Black Expo's year-round schedule of events, which also includes the Summer Celebration.

500 Festival Parade
www.500festival.com

Circle City Classic
www.circlecityclassic.com

Circle City IN Pride Festival and Parade
www.circlecityinpride.org

GO WILD
AT THE INDIANAPOLIS ZOO

Take a trip around the world at the Indianapolis Zoo, which is home to more than 250 animal species. One highlight is the International Orangutan Center: the rainforest-like environment houses nine orangutans, giving them plenty of space to climb. Buy a ticket for the Skyline gondola ride to get an aerial view of the orangutans' habitat.

Next, flock to Flights of Fancy. This exhibit consists of three walk-through aviaries, including one where you can feed birdseed to colorful budgies. The Oceans exhibit also has interactive options, including a shark petting tank and lively dolphin shows. (If you plan ahead, you can schedule a time to swim with the dolphins.) The Deserts Dome is home to meerkats and lizards, and the Forests Biome houses tigers, lemurs, and bears. The largest section is the Plains Biome, where you'll find African animals, such as zebras, giraffes, rhinos, cheetahs, lions, and elephants. Oh my.

1200 W. Washington St., 317-630-2001
www.indianapoliszoo.com

SEE THE STARS
AT THE HOLCOMB OBSERVATORY AND PLANETARIUM

When night falls on the campus of Butler University, the domed tower of Holcomb Observatory casts a gentle glow across the quiet lawns. Constructed in 1954, the observatory is open for public tours on most Friday and Saturday evenings during the school year. There's no charge to gaze through Indiana's largest telescope, which recently underwent a $425,000 refurbishment. Tour guides, who are usually astronomy students, point out such objects as planets, the moon, and star clusters. The supplementary planetarium show costs a measly three dollars (cash only). In other words, it's one of the cheapest dates in town. Just keep an eye on the weather forecast. Viewings are canceled when heavy cloud cover limits visibility.

4600 Sunset Ave., 317-940-8333
www.butler.edu/holcomb-observatory

TAKE A ROAD TRIP
TO ARCHITECTURAL LANDMARKS IN COLUMBUS, INDIANA

Located halfway between Indianapolis and Louisville, Columbus is an unlikely place for a mecca of modernist architecture. But the city owes a debt to the late J. Irwin Miller, former chairman of the Columbus-based Cummins corporation. In the 1950s, he made a deal with the city: the Cummins Foundation paid big-name modernist architects to design new schools, libraries, and other public buildings, thus populating the city with noteworthy architecture.

For his own home, Miller enlisted renowned architect Eero Saarinen, best known for St. Louis's iconic Gateway Arch. Today, the Miller House and Garden is one of the best-preserved modernist homes in the nation, and it is curated by the Indianapolis Museum of Art. To sign up for a tour, contact the Columbus Area Visitors Center, which also coordinates tours of the city's other architectural highlights.

Columbus Area Visitors Center, 506 Fifth St., Columbus, 800-468-6564
www.columbus.in.us

EXPLORE INDY'S
MUSEUM CAMPUS

White River State Park is a scenic spot for a picnic, but it's also home to several popular museums. Start your museum-hopping day at the Indiana State Museum, which highlights the state's natural and cultural history. Let yourself be mesmerized by the gentle swing of the Foucault pendulum, which demonstrates the Earth's rotation, and then look for sculptures from all ninety-two Indiana counties embedded in the museum's facade and walkways. Nearby is the Eiteljorg Museum of American Indians and Western Art, which has one of the world's top collections of contemporary Native American art. Finally, head to the NCAA Hall of Champions, which celebrates collegiate sports with two floors of interactive exhibits and video highlights. White River State Park is also home to the Indianapolis Zoo and Victory Field.

Eiteljorg Museum of American Indians and Western Art
500 W. Washington St., 317-636-9378
www.eiteljorg.org

Indiana State Museum
650 W. Washington St., 317-232-1637
www.indianamuseum.org

NCAA Hall of Champions
700 W. Washington St., 317-916-4255
www.ncaahallofchampions.org

EXPERIENCE
THE UNDERGROUND RAILROAD AT FOLLOW THE NORTH STAR AT CONNER PRAIRIE

You've read about slavery in textbooks. You've seen it depicted in movies. But you'll never understand its true horror until you experience it—or at least a tiny piece of it—firsthand. That's why Conner Prairie, an interactive history park, developed Follow the North Star. The program puts you in the shoes of a fugitive slave on the Underground Railroad. Your journey begins at a slave auction in 1836, where you'll be demeaned and quizzed about your skills. Your new owners will laugh at you as you perform menial tasks. Then your moment of escape will come. But will you make it to freedom? Who will help you along the way, and who will hinder your journey? The two-hour program is emotionally intense, so it's not for young children, and even adults may need to opt out partway through. But try to stick with it. It isn't fun, but it is unforgettable.

13400 Allisonville Rd., Fishers, 317-776-6000
www.connerprairie.org

FIVE MORE REASONS TO VISIT CONNER PRAIRIE

Conner Prairie, Indiana's only Smithsonian-affiliated institution, is an interactive history park focusing on Indiana life in the 1800s. You can stroll through a pioneer village and homestead in 1836, experience the Civil War in 1863, and explore a Native American encampment—all with a bounty of activities for children. Here are five more reasons to visit:

1. Board a tethered hot-air balloon in the 1859 Balloon Voyage exhibit and soar 350 feet above the surrounding landscape.

2. From January to March, experience the Hearthside Suppers program, where you'll cook authentic recipes the old-fashioned way and share a meal with other participants.

3. In October, celebrate Halloween with the Headless Horseman. Conner Prairie offers haunted hayrides, kid-friendly activities, and an apple store filled with seasonal treats.

4. In December, try Conner Prairie by Candlelight. You'll stroll through Prairietown after dark, stopping at each house to hear costumed interpreters describe historic holiday traditions. It's the best way I know to reconnect with the simple joys of the holiday season.

5. See the Indianapolis Symphony Orchestra perform under the stars at Symphony on the Prairie.

TAKE AN ART CLASS
AT THE INDIANAPOLIS ART CENTER

The Indianapolis Art Center is, without question, the best place in town to take an art class. The center has large studios for glassblowing, art welding, photography, and woodworking, and its instructors excel at teaching painting, drawing, ceramics, jewelry-making, weaving, and other skills. Plunge in with a university-style class that spans seven or fifteen weeks, giving you a chance to create multiple projects. Not ready to commit? Try a weekend workshop or a two-hour pop-up class focused on a specific project, such as a glass paperweight or metal bracelet. The Art Center also has classes for children and teenagers, including weeklong summer camps.

820 E. Sixty-Seventh St., 317-255-2464
www.indplsartcenter.org

TIP
Looking for a unique gift? The juried Broad Ripple Art Fair, held each May on the campus of the Indianapolis Art Center, showcases the region's best artists and artisans in a fun atmosphere, complete with live music and beer tastings.

HUNT FOR PUBLIC ART
WITH THE INDY ARTS GUIDE

The Indy Arts Guide, which is maintained by the Arts Council of Indianapolis, lists hundreds of pieces of public art throughout the city. Your mission is to discover your favorites. You'll find several iconic pieces in the Massachusetts Avenue Cultural District. Julian Opie's *Ann Dancing* is an electronic sign featuring a swaying female figure. Nearby is James Tyler's *Brickhead 3*, a large human head made of bricks. And you can't miss *My Affair with Kurt Vonnegut*, an enormous mural created by artist Pamela Bliss to memorialize the late hometown author.

My personal favorites are four cute sculptures by Tom Otterness, purchased after a temporary installation of Otterness sculptures throughout the city in 2005. *Boy and Dog* resides at the corner of East and St. Clair streets, just steps from Mass Ave. Three other pieces, *Free Money*, *Female Tourist*, and *Male Tourist*, live in front of the Indiana Convention Center.

www.indyartsguide.org/public-art

COMMUNE WITH KILGORE TROUT
AT THE KURT VONNEGUT MUSEUM AND LIBRARY

The late author Kurt Vonnegut said, "All my jokes are Indianapolis. All my attitudes are Indianapolis. My adenoids are Indianapolis. If I ever severed myself from Indianapolis, I would be out of business. What people like about me is Indianapolis." Fortunately, Indianapolis likes Kurt Vonnegut right back. The Kurt Vonnegut Museum and Library celebrates the hometown author's numerous works, such as *Slaughterhouse Five*, *Breakfast of Champions*, and *Sirens of Titan*. The library displays Vonnegut memorabilia and a fascinating timeline of his life, and it doubles as an art gallery; a few of Vonnegut's own doodles are always on display. You can click away on a typewriter just like the one Vonnegut owned (and see the real thing behind glass), view candid photos donated by his family members, and chuckle over the many rejection letters he received from editors who should have known better. Note: Check the address before you go. The museum is actively seeking a new, permanent location.

340 N. Senate Ave.
www.vonnegutlibrary.org

80

CELEBRATE AFRICAN AMERICAN CULTURE
AT INDIANA BLACK EXPO'S
SUMMER CELEBRATION

Held each July, Indiana Black Expo's Summer Celebration is the state's premier showcase of African American culture and one of the largest festivals of ethnic culture in the nation. The ten-day schedule includes concerts, fashion shows, and an enormous exhibition hall, where vendors sell everything from hair-care products to health insurance. The Summer Celebration also includes community-focused events, such as health fairs and educational workshops. Can't make it to the Summer Celebration? Mark your calendar instead for IBE's Circle City Classic. The annual October football game highlights two historically black colleges or universities, with coinciding pageants, concerts, and parades.

www.indianablackexpo.com

SNEAK A PEEK AT ARTISTS' STUDIOS
AT THE STUTZ ARTISTS OPEN HOUSE

In the early 1900s, when Indianapolis was a hub for auto manufacturing, the Stutz Motor Company churned out speedy sports cars, such as the Bearcat and the Blackhawk. Now its former downtown factory houses more than eighty artists' studios—the Midwest's largest group of artists working under one roof. The four-hundred-thousand-square-foot complex spans an entire city block, and it can seem a bit intimidating. So the annual two-day open house is a welcome chance to explore. Usually held in April, the event highlights members of the Stutz Artists Association, who sell artwork and give tours of their studio spaces. You'll find everything from delicate beaded earrings to hulking pieces of furniture. Alas, the sleek vintage cars are for display only, not for sale.

212 W. Tenth St.
www.stutzartists.com

SEE A TRULY MOVING PICTURE
AT THE HEARTLAND FILM FESTIVAL

It's not quite Cannes, but each October Indy's Heartland Film Festival brings together independent filmmakers from across the globe. Over a ten-day period, the festival offers public screenings of about 130 films, which is less than 10 percent of the films submitted to the festival for consideration. The festival's reputation for feel-good films isn't quite accurate; its real focus is "purposeful" filmmaking that educates and inspires, not just entertains. You might see documentaries about the civil rights movement or women's unequal representation as orchestra conductors, narrative features about cattle rustlers or California folk musicians, or an animated film about a young Swazi girl searching for her brothers. And you might meet some of the world's top filmmakers along the way.

1043 Virginia Ave., 317-464-9405
www.heartlandfilm.org/festival

CLIMB A GIANT SKELETON
AT 100 ACRES: THE VIRGINIA B. FAIRBANKS ART AND NATURE PARK

Curated by the Indianapolis Museum of Art, 100 Acres is one of the largest museum-owned art parks in the nation. Commissioned artists install large, site-responsive sculptures in the park's quiet forests and meadows, so there's always a surprise around the next curve in the walking path. Fans of John Green's *The Fault in Our Stars* will recognize *Funky Bones*, Atelier Van Lieshout's giant skeleton sculpture. Other favorites include *Free Basket*, a basketball court covered in the arcs of bouncing balls; *Align*, a pair of suspended rings whose shadows meet only on the summer solstice; and a series of eye-catching steel benches. Yes, you can touch the art. In fact, you probably should.

4000 Michigan Rd., 317-923-1331
www.discovernewfields.org

FIGURE OUT A FRINGE SCHEDULE
AT THE INDYFRINGE THEATER FESTIVAL

To understand the magic of the IndyFringe theater festival, you have to do some math: eleven days + eight stages + more than sixty performing arts groups = nearly four hundred experimental performances, starting every hour, on the hour, from early afternoon to late evening. All the venues are within the Massachusetts Avenue Cultural District, so you can walk from show to show, chatting with performers and other theatergoers along the way. Shows last about forty-five minutes and cost ten dollars each, with discounts available for ticket packages. The hard part is setting your schedule. In one day, you can see a wacky new musical about bowling pins, a reinterpretation of a Greek or Shakespearean classic, a family-friendly magic show, a raunchy stand-up comedy act, a dance performance, and a choral concert. You may encounter a few clunkers along the way, but even those are sure to be memorable.

www.indyfringe.org

GET DRAMATIC
WITH INDY'S THEATER SCENE

In recent years, the Indy theater scene has finally stepped out of Chicago's long shadow. The new Indianapolis Shakespeare Company brings plays to local parks, while the recently expanded IndyFringe Theatre offers a lineup that's delightfully quirky—not to mention its huge annual festival. And the Phoenix Theatre, formerly housed in an old church, recently moved to a purpose-built space. It's best known for offbeat musicals like *Fun Home, Urinetown*, and *Naked Boys Singing,* as well as its hilarious Christmas show. But there's challenging drama here too, from *The Cripple of Inishmaan to August: Osage County.* For a more consistently straight-laced production, try the Indiana Repertory Theatre. Recent plays have included *Noises Off, The Curious Incident of the Dog in the Night-Time,* and *A Raisin in the Sun,* and its annual production of *A Christmas Carol* is a holiday tradition for many families.

Indiana Repertory Theatre, 140 W. Washington St., 317-635-5252
www.irtlive.com

Phoenix Theatre, 705 N. Illinois St., 317-635-7529
www.phoenixtheatre.org

SEE SHAKESPEARE
UNDER THE STARS

Quality productions of Shakespeare's plays can be hard to come by in Indy, so the Indianapolis Shakespeare Company is a breath of fresh air. Each summer, the company's professional actors mount a Shakespeare production, such as *Othello* or *As You Like It*, in a local park. The actors take their work seriously, but the atmosphere is casual: picnicking is encouraged, admission is free, and families are welcome—as are Comic Con attendees still wearing their Pokémon costumes (true story). On surveys, many attendees report that they've never seen any play before, let alone a Shakespeare play, but the talented actors can ease even the most reluctant playgoers into the rhythm of Shakespeare's language. The magic of Indy Shakes is that it trusts its audiences to rise to the challenge—and, year after year, they do.

www.indyshakes.com

TAKE A CEMETERY TOUR
AT CROWN HILL CEMETERY

Crown Hill Cemetery, which opened in 1864, is the third-largest cemetery in the nation. It's the final resting place of nearly two hundred thousand people, including Civil War general Jefferson Davis, Depression-era bank robber John Dillinger, President Benjamin Harrison, poet James Whitcomb Riley, and novelist Booth Tarkington. Riley's monument is a perfect spot for a sunset picnic; it sits atop the highest hill in Marion County, offering a great view of the downtown skyline.

A guided tour is the best way to appreciate Crown Hill. Start with the ninety-minute Heritage Tour, which covers the cemetery's history and Gothic architecture. Other tours focus on specific groups of "residents," such as Civil War personalities, African Americans, women, authors, and veterans. Or, try the Skeletons in the Closet tour to get good dirt on Indy's former residents.

700 W. Thirty-Eighth St., 317-920-2644
www.crownhill.org

JOIN
THE FIRST FRIDAY FRENZY

Indy's art galleries and studios draw their biggest crowds during First Friday art tours. Originally an initiative of the Indianapolis Downtown Artists and Dealers Association (now dissolved), the First Fridays concept soon took on a life of its own. The geographic focal point has shifted with the times—when rents rose in the Mass Ave and Fountain Square neighborhoods, artists fled to new hot spots. One is the Circle City Industrial Complex, a five-hundred-thousand-square-foot facility that houses forty artist studios, a winter farmers' market, a brewery, a pottery studio, and local favorite Lick Ice Cream. Another hot spot is the Garfield Park neighborhood, especially the Tube Factory Artspace, home of the influential Big Car artists collective. Don't know where to start? The Arts Council of Indianapolis's online Indy Arts Guide does a good job of compiling upcoming First Friday happenings, from exhibition openings and curator talks to meet-the-artist events.

Circle City Industrial Complex, 1125 Brookside Ave.
www.circlecityind.com

Indy Arts Guide
www.indyartsguide.org

Tube Factory Artspace, 1125 S. Cruft St.
www.bigcar.org

PICNIC
AT THE RUINS AT HOLLIDAY PARK

Encompassing ninety-four acres, Holliday Park offers the usual mix of playgrounds, picnic areas, and walking trails. But it does have one unique feature, the Ruins, which makes you feel like you're picnicking in Athens or Rome. Its three large sculptures, called *The Races of Man,* were rescued from the facade of New York's St. Paul Building before its demolition in the 1950s. The building's owner wanted to save the statues, which were then valued at about $150,000. So it held a design competition, asking cities to submit proposals for putting the statues on permanent display. Indy's winning plan mimicked the facade of the St. Paul Building, thus placing the statues in their original context. In the end, it was something of a homecoming for the statues, which were carved from Indiana limestone. Pack a picnic basket and go say hello.

6363 Spring Mill Rd., 317-327-7180
www.hollidaypark.org

SAMPLE THE SUMMER NIGHTS FILM SERIES
AT THE INDIANAPOLIS MUSEUM OF ART

On Friday evenings in summer, bring a blanket and your favorite picnic fare to the outdoor terrace at the Indianapolis Museum of Art. As part of its Summer Nights film series, the museum screens classic films like *Vertigo* and *Breakfast at Tiffany's*, as well as newer favorites like *Dirty Dancing* and *The Princess Bride*. Trust me, you haven't seen *Dirty Dancing* properly until you've seen it under the stars, glass of wine in hand, surrounded by a crowd of people who cheer when Baby finally pulls off that lift. Tickets often sell out, so be sure to book early.

Looking for a winter activity instead? Check out the Winter Nights film series, which takes place in the museum's indoor theater, affectionately called the Toby. It offers the same mix of classic favorites and contemporary hits.

4000 Michigan Rd., 317-923-1331
www.discovernewfields.org

SIX MORE REASONS TO VISIT THE IMA

The Indianapolis Museum of Art is an institution in transition, and recent changes—charging a new admission fee, attempting to rebrand the sprawling campus as "Newfields," and closing public access to popular bike paths—have alienated many locals. That said, you'll still find many things to do at this important cultural asset, including the following:

1. Snap a photo with Robert Indiana's iconic *LOVE* sculpture—recently moved indoors to protect it from the elements.

2. Explore the IMA's newly refurbished Design Gallery, the nation's largest museum showcase of modern and contemporary design, from mid-century furniture to Dyson vacuum cleaners.

3. Climb outdoor sculptures and spy on nesting birds at 100 Acres: The Virginia B. Fairbanks Art and Nature Park.

4. Come to "Indiana's nicest day," the annual Penrod Arts Fair, held each September on the IMA grounds.

5. During the holidays, walk through an outdoor wonderland of lights—more than a million of them—at the Winterlights event.

6. Play the temporary putt-putt course, redesigned each summer by local artists. Each hole celebrates a piece of Indiana history, like the 1822 squirrel stampede.

PAY HOMAGE
AT INDY'S WAR MEMORIALS

Fun fact: Washington, DC, is the only city in the nation with more war memorials than Indianapolis. One highlight is the Indiana War Memorial Plaza, a cluster of neoclassical monuments honoring local veterans of World War II, the Vietnam War, and the Korean War. To the north and south, the plaza is bookended by the American Legion's national headquarters and the Indiana War Memorial, which has a nifty military museum inside. Along the nearby Canal Walk, you'll find memorials to the USS *Indianapolis*, which was torpedoed in 1945, and to recipients of the Congressional Medal of Honor. And don't forget the Soldiers and Sailors Monument on Monument Circle; it honors veterans of earlier conflicts, including the Civil War.

A WALKING TOUR: INDY'S WAR MEMORIALS

Start your journey at the Soldiers and Sailors Monument and head north on Meridian Street to Indiana War Memorial Plaza. After you look around, go west on Michigan Street to the Canal Walk. Turn right for the USS *Indianapolis* Memorial, and then double back along the Canal Walk toward the Congressional Medal of Honor Memorial, which is sandwiched between Military Park and White River State Park. If you loop back to Monument Circle afterward, the itinerary is just less than three miles and takes about ninety minutes, depending on how long you linger at each site.

Photo Courtesy of Molly Mayer

SHOPPING
AND FASHION

HANDPICK SOME HANDMADE GOODS
AT THE INDIEana HANDICRAFT EXCHANGE

If the words "craft fair" make you think of Martha Stewart, think again. The INDIEana Handicraft Exchange—held each June at the Harrison Center for the Arts—is a showcase of fun, functional, and decidedly modern handmade goods. Check out stained-glass suncatchers modeled on tattoo designs, wooden cutting boards inspired by vintage video games, and calendars that double as anatomical coloring books.

When you're ready for a break, grab a bite to eat at one of the food trucks lining Delaware Street, or sample such local treats as gourmet marshmallows from 240sweet, Newfangled Confections' addictive fudge-meets-brittle Frittle candy, and fun flavored popcorn from Just Pop In.

Don't despair if the summer INDIEana Handicraft Exchange doesn't fit your schedule. There's a smaller Winter Market each December, and the event's organizers carry many of the same items year-round at their Mass Ave boutique, Homespun: Modern Handmade.

www.indieanahandicraftexchange.com

MEET THE FINEST HOOSIER ARTISANS
AT THE INDIANA ARTISAN MARKETPLACE

The Indiana Artisan program recognizes the state's top makers, from woodworkers to sculptors to cheesemakers. The juried program isn't just a rubber stamp for handmade goods; it's a seal of approval awarded to only a small fraction of the artisans who apply. The annual Indiana Artisan Marketplace, held each spring at the Indiana State Fairgrounds, showcases the work of more than three hundred approved artisans. Shop for unique artwork, pretty paper goods, eye-catching jewelry, crave-worthy food products, and the state's best beers and wines. You won't find many bargains here. Instead, come prepared to splurge on a one-of-a-kind piece that you'll treasure for a lifetime.

www.indianaartisan.org

SNAG
A TRENDY ANTIQUE

Whether you're looking for antique Ball jars or sleek mid-century furniture, you'll find something to suit your style at the Indie Arts and Vintage Marketplace. The upscale monthly market is held at different locations throughout the city, bringing together dozens of vendors specializing in stylish vintage and antique goods.

Still more vintage wares are available at the city's antique stores. Society of Salvage, which gives new life to "modern vintage" objects, is a hipster favorite. The largest shop is the Midland Arts and Antiques Market, where two sprawling floors of vendor booths contain everything from junky ceramics to high-end furniture. These vendors are savvy, so you won't find many bargains here. Instead, you may find a unique piece that you suddenly realize you can't live without. I have a hideously amazing mushroom-shaped cookie jar to prove it.

Indie Arts and Vintage Marketplace, www.indyartsvintage.com

Midland Arts and Antiques Market, 907 E. Michigan St., 317-267-9005
www.midlandathome.com

Society of Salvage, 1021 E. Michigan St., 317-964-0513
www.societyofsalvage.com

BE A WORD NERD
AT INDY'S INDEPENDENT BOOKSTORES

Ignore the grim predictions: Indy's independent bookstores are thriving, not only as shops but also as event venues. One popular option is Indy Reads Books, a cozy used bookstore on Mass Ave whose profits support adult literacy programs. It's a hot spot for book signings and readings, so keep an eye on the calendar.

Meanwhile, Books and Brews—now with seven locations in the metro area—is rapidly building an empire. The house beers, such as the Charlie and the Chocolate Stout, are named for beloved books, and each location doubles as tasting room and used bookstore. Check the calendar for open mic nights, trivia, live music, and other events.

If you're shopping for the little ones, try Kids Ink. This children's bookstore, which also stocks puzzles and games, schedules regular story hours and author visits. Bonus: Kids will love the Flying Cupcake bakery next door.

Books and Brews, multiple locations
www.booksnbrews.com

Indy Reads Books, 911 Massachusetts Ave., 317-384-1496
www.indyreadsbooks.org

Kids Ink Children's Bookstore, 5619 N. Illinois St., 317-255-2598
www.kidsinkbooks.com

SHOP
BROAD RIPPLE

By night, Broad Ripple's overflowing bars give the neighborhood a frat-party feel. But by day, the neighborhood retains its family-friendly village charm, offering a quirky mix of shops. Fuel up with a latte from Hubbard and Cravens and stroll east along Broad Ripple Avenue, stopping to browse at shops like Pitaya and Indy CD and Vinyl. Next, turn left on Guilford Avenue, where you'll find the Just Pop In popcorn shop and the Artifacts Gallery, a showcase of artisan goods. The next cross street is Westfield Boulevard, home to the eclectic Bungalow shop and an ever-changing roster of women's clothing boutiques. Don't be afraid to venture onto the side streets, where you'll find shops selling vintage clothing, French pastries, hiking gear, and more. When you need a break, you'll have plenty of options, from all-natural popsicles at Nicey Pop Shop to pints of lager at Broad Ripple Brewpub.

Artifacts Gallery
6327 Guilford Ave.
317-255-1178
www.artifactsindy.com

Broad Ripple Brewpub
842 E. Sixty-Fifth St.
317-253-2739
www.broadripplebrewpub.com

Bungalow
924 E. Westfield Blvd.
317-253-5028
www.facebook.com/thebungalowinc

Indy CD and Vinyl
806 Broad Ripple Ave.
317-259-1012
www.indycdandvinyl.com

Just Pop In
6302 N. Guilford Ave.
317-257-9338
www.justpopinonline.com

Nicey Pop Shop
916 E. Westfield Blvd.
317-602-6423
www.niceytreat.com

Pitaya
842 Broad Ripple Ave.
317-465-0000
www.pitaya.com

SHOP
DOWNTOWN ZIONSVILLE

Downtown Zionsville's brick streets are lined with quaint nineteenth-century buildings, so shopping in this Indianapolis suburb feels like stepping back in time. The village has its share of antique stores and cluttered gift shops, but that's not all. Ballerinas and Bruisers carries cute children's clothing, Ganache Chocolatier sells exquisite gourmet truffles, and Lesley Jane specializes in women's clothing. The Village Yarn Company is a cheerful place to browse, even if you're not a knitter. I love searching the stacks at Black Dog Books and exploring local art at the Art IN Hand Gallery. But my favorite thing about downtown Zionsville is the food and drink, such as wine milkshakes at Hopwood Cellars and thick slices of Mom's Original Dutch Apple Pie at My Sugar Pie.

Art IN Hand Gallery
211 S. Main St., Zionsville, 317-733-8426
www.artinhandgallery.com

Ballerinas and Bruisers
180 S. Main St., Zionsville, 317-733-3400
www.ballerinasandbruisers.com

Black Dog Books
115 S. Main St., Zionsville, 317-733-1747
www.blackdogbooksin.com

Ganache Chocolatier
55 E. Pine St., Zionsville, 317-873-6948
www.ganache.com

Hopwood Cellars
12 E. Cedar St., Zionsville, 317-873-4099
www.hopwoodcellars.com

Lesley Jane
150 S. Main St., Zionsville, 317-873-9999
www.lesleyjane.com

My Sugar Pie
40 E. Pine St., Zionsville, 317-733-8717
www.mysugarpie.com

Village Yarn Company
209 S. Main St., Zionsville, 317-873-0004
www.villageyarncompany.wordpress.com

SHOP
THE MASSACHUSETTS AVENUE CULTURAL DISTRICT

Block for block, diagonal Mass Ave has more restaurants, boutiques, cultural attractions, and public art than anywhere else in the city. Start your shopping trip at Stout's Footwear, the nation's oldest shoe store. On the 400 block, kids and parents alike will love Nurture, a baby boutique. Silver in the City is a top pick for quirky housewares, gifts, and jewelry, and Global Gifts stocks fair trade artisan wares from around the world. Next, take a quick detour to Walnut Street, where Chatham Home Interiors carries eclectic home decor. Then head northeast to the 800 block, home to Best Chocolate in Town; the Art Bank gallery; Crimson Tate, a modern fabric store; Homespun: Modern Handmade; and Mass Ave Wine. One block farther you'll find Indy Reads Books, one of my favorite places to browse for new and used titles. Just be sure to take breaks in the cupcake shops, restaurants, and cocktail bars along the way.

TIP
Crimson Tate has a full schedule of hip, fun classes, from Sewing 101 to classes focused on projects like tote bags, iPad cases, and basic quilts. This isn't your grandmother's fabric store.

www.crimsontate.com

Art Bank
811 Massachusetts Ave.
317-624-1010
www.artbankgallery.com

Best Chocolate in Town
880 Massachusetts Ave.
317-636-2800
www.bestchocolateintown.com

Chatham Home Interiors
517 E. Walnut St.
317-917-8550
www.chathamhomeindy.com

Crimson Tate
845 Massachusetts Ave.
317-426-3300
www.crimsontate.com

Global Gifts
446 Massachusetts Ave.
317-423-3148
www.globalgiftsft.com

Homespun:
Modern Handmade
869 Massachusetts Ave.
317-351-0280
www.homespunindy.com

Indy Reads Books
911 Massachusetts Ave.
317-384-1496
www.indyreadsbooks.org

Mass Ave Wine
878 Massachusetts Ave.
317-972-7966
www.massavewine.com

Nurture
433 Massachusetts Ave.
317-423-1234
www.nurtureonline.com

Silver in the City
434 Massachusetts Ave.
317-955-9925
www.silverinthecity.com

Stout's Footwear
318 Massachusetts Ave.
317-632-7818
www.stoutsfootwear.com

SHOP THE CARMEL
ARTS AND DESIGN DISTRICT

Carmel may be located just north of Indianapolis, but it's no mere suburb. The city has fought hard—and spent millions—to maintain its own identity, investing in projects like the Center for the Performing Arts and the flourishing downtown Arts and Design District. The area is packed with high-end art galleries, interior design showrooms, upscale clothing boutiques, and restaurants. The neighborhood flagship is the Indiana Design Center, a regional hub for interior design. It houses two art galleries, several artist studios, and the offices of nineteen interior design firms. Its fifteen showrooms exhibit the latest in flooring, furniture, kitchen and bath design, interior decor, and home automation. Showrooms on the first floor are open to the public; the ones upstairs are for industry professionals only. If you need guidance or inspiration, try the center's free "designer on call" service.

Carmel Arts and Design District
www.carmelartsanddesign.com

Indiana Design Center
200 S. Rangeline Rd., Carmel, 317-569-5975
www.indianadesigncenter.com

GRAB THE PERFECT HOLIDAY GIFT
AT YELP'S TOTALLY BAZAAR

The city's hippest pop-up shopping party takes place each December, just in time to pick out last-minute holiday gifts. Yelp gathers together more than one hundred central Indiana artisans selling everything from handcrafted jewelry to gourmet peanut butter. It's the perfect place to find Indy-centric gifts: Historic Indianapolis sells frame-worthy posters, and People for Urban Progress offers limited-edition snowflake ornaments made from scraps of the former RCA Dome's canvas roof. Meanwhile, DJs spin trendy tunes, local breweries and wineries serve their wares, and food trucks line up on the streets outside. No one will judge you if you decide to buy a few little gifts for yourself too.

www.yelp.com/events

SUGGESTED ITINERARIES

ACTIVE OUTDOOR ADVENTURES

CULTURAL AFFAIRS

• •

ESSENTIAL INDIANAPOLIS

• •

FAMILY FUN

FOOD FINDS

FREEBIES

• •

HISTORY LESSONS

ROMANTIC RENDEZVOUS

• •

SPORTS SPOTS

EVENTS BY SEASON

SPRING

SUMMER

FALL

WINTER

INDEX

• •